CONVERSION
IN THE
NEW TESTAMENT

Ronald D. Witherup, S.S.

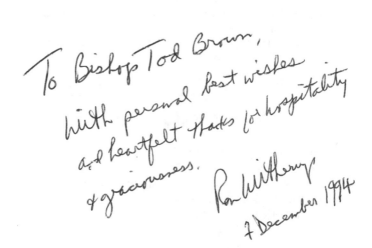

To Bishop Tod Brown, with personal best wishes and heartfelt thanks for hospitality & graciousness.

Ron Witherup
7 December 1994

A Michael Glazier Book
THE LITURGICAL PRESS
Collegeville, Minnesota

Zacchaeus Studies: New Testament

General Editor: Mary Ann Getty

A Michael Glazier Book published by The Liturgical Press

Cover design by David Manahan, O.S.B.
St. Paul, Fra Bartolommeo (1475–1517), Pinacoteca, Vatican Museum.

1   2   3   4   5   6   7   8

Library of Congress Cataloging-in-Publication Data

Witherup, Ronald D., 1950–
    Conversion in the New Testament / Ronald D. Witherup.
        p.   cm. — (Zacchaeus studies.   New Testament)
    "A Michael Glazier book."
    Includes bibliographical references.
    ISBN 0-8146-5837-7
    1. Conversion—Biblical teaching. 2. Bible. N.T.—Criticism, interpretation, etc. I. Title. II. Series.
    BS2545.C59W586   1994
    248.2'4'09015—dc20   93-28774
                                                           CIP

To David and Rose,
who first taught me the
necessity of ongoing conversion

Contents

Editor's Note

Zacchaeus Studies provide concise, readable and relatively inexpensive scholarly studies on particular aspects of scripture and theology. The New Testament section of the series presents studies dealing with focal or debated questions; and the volumes focus on specific texts or particular themes of current interest in biblical interpretation. Specialists have their professional journals and other forums where they discuss matters of mutual concern, exchange ideas and further contemporary trends of research; and some of their work on contemporary biblical research is now made accessible for students and others in *Zacchaeus Studies*.

The authors in this series share their own scholarship in non-technical language, in the areas of their expertise and interest. These writers stand with the best in current biblical scholarship in the English-speaking world. Since most of them are teachers, they are accustomed to presenting difficult material in comprehensible form without compromising a high level of critical judgment and analysis.

The works of this series are ecumenical in content and purpose and cross credal boundaries. They are designed to augment formal and informal biblical study and discussion. Hopefully they will also serve as texts to enhance and supplement seminary, university and college classes. The series will also aid Bible study groups, adult education and parish religious education classes to develop intelligent, versatile and challenging programs for those they serve.

Mary Ann Getty
New Testament Editor

Acknowledgments

Unless otherwise noted, biblical quotations are taken from the New American Bible, copyright © 1970 and from the New American Bible With Revised New Testament, copyright © 1986 by the Confraternity of Christian Doctrine, 3211 Fourth St. N.E., Washington, DC 20017-1194 and are used by permission of the copyright holder. All rights reserved.

The author is also grateful to the editor of *The Bible Today* for permission to use a revised version of "Conversion in Mark" (ch. 2) which originally appeared in that journal.

Abbreviations

AB	Anchor Bible
Bib	*Biblica*
ETL	*Ephemerides theologicae lovanienses*
JBL	*Journal of Biblical Literature*
JSNT	*Journal for the Study of the New Testament*
JSNTSup	Journal for the Study of the New Testament — Supplement Series
LXX	Septuagint
NTS	*New Testament Studies*
RelSRev	*Religious Studies Review*
SBLDS	Society of Biblical Literature Dissertation Series
TDNT	G. Kittel and G. Friedrich (eds.), *Theological Dictionary of the New Testament*
TS	*Theological Studies*
WUNT	Wissenschaftliche Untersuchungen zum Neuen Testament
ZTK	*Zeitschrift für Theologie und Kirche*

Introduction

Conversion is "in" again. Interest in the topic extends to a broad spectrum of individuals. On the one hand, theologians like Bernard Lonergan have sparked interest in sophisticated analyses of conversion from a variety of perspectives, such as its intellectual, religious, and moral horizons. The psychological and anthropological dimensions of conversion are especially attractive to many people who seek to study the phenomenon from a scientific point of view. On the other hand, simplistic, jargon-filled analyses can be found among the ranks of many Bible-toting Christians. Evangelicals and charismatics regularly challenge other Christians with the sharply intoned question, "Have you been born again?" Politicians and TV evangelists invoke recent "conversion" experiences to justify the public's forgiveness of one wrongdoing or another, especially if it helps a floundering career. Twelve step programs, such as Alcoholics Anonymous, indicate that they can totally change a person's life by effecting a turnabout, a conversion, that moves one from some type of dependency and codependency to a healthy, adult life.[1]

Behind all this talk of conversion is the underlying assumption that everyone knows what conversion is and what it means, especially if you are a Bible-believing Christian. Most Christians think it axiomatic to assert that conversion is central to the message of Jesus. But does the New Testament (hereafter, NT), especially in the Gospels, describe Christian conversion in a uniform manner? What do the Gospels really say about conversion? Do they, in fact, have a common understanding of this notion? In what ways does the rest of the NT nuance the notion of conversion?

1

The purpose of this book is to explore thoroughly the theme of conversion in the NT. In keeping with the *Zacchaeus Studies* format, it is intended for general audiences and is designed to give an overview of the topic while leading readers to other resources for further study. Footnotes are kept to a minimum and generally refer to works not listed in the selected bibliography. While many books have been written in recent years on the broad topic of conversion, it has been thirty years since the appearance of a small, popular monograph on the specific topic of the biblical description of conversion (Hulsbosch 1966; Dutch original 1963). Most contemporary studies have been theological or psychological in orientation, with only modest exposition of the biblical data. Consequently, much has been written about the types of conversions, or the psychology of them, or the mechanisms which produce them, but lacking is an appreciation of the breadth of NT teaching. This study seeks to provide such a resource.

Methodological and Organizational Considerations

There are different ways to conceive of this project. I could have chosen to do a *historical* study which would have attempted to describe the development of the notion of conversion in early Christian history. Such a study would have necessitated going from the earliest NT data (Paul's genuine letters) to the latest NT books (Revelation and 2 Peter). Instead, I have chosen to write a *thematic* study. The reason is simple. After careful consideration I have come to believe that the NT shows a fairly uniform teaching about conversion with minimal evidence for a dramatic evolution of the concept. An equally strong conviction, however, is that it shows an incredibly broad way of understanding conversion, much broader than the average Christian is likely to assume. A thematic study places emphasis on the breadth of description while not necessarily ignoring developmental and historical issues. Moreover, a thematic study need not be restricted to a mere concordance examination of the technical language of conversion. As we shall see, the NT understanding goes beyond typical, technical conversion language in a variety of ways.

The choice of method helped to dictate the outline of the book. In nine chapters we will explore all the major aspects of the NT on conversion, including its debt to the Old Testament (hereafter, OT). After an initial chapter on linguistic evidence, we will start with the Gospels and proceed through the other NT materials. With regard to the Synoptic Gospels, I operate out of the majority scholarly view that Mark is the earliest Gospel, followed by Matthew and Luke, though this theory is not critical to the understanding offered herein. I refer the reader to a standard NT introduction or one-volume commentary for basic information regarding authorship, date, provenance, etc. of the various NT books.[2] The Acts of the Apostles is considered immediately after Luke's Gospel because of their common authorship and thematic relationship. Then we explore in separate chapters the Gospel of John and the Pauline letters (genuine and Deutero-Pauline). Finally, the remaining NT books are treated collectively because of the relative scarcity of information on conversion. The final chapter attempts to synthesize the NT evidence about conversion into a "biblical theology" that serves as a foundation for understanding Christian conversion.

Conversion as a Modern Problem

To claim that conversion is a modern problem may seem peculiar. But in the last decade of the twentieth century, with "born againism" on the rise and people desperately in search of some normative religious values in life, conversion is indeed a problem. Let me explain.

When I announced to some friends that I was writing a book on conversion in the NT, they immediately wanted to know which stories of individual conversions I would include. They automatically associated the term "conversion" with the Acts of the Apostles and with stories of individuals throughout history who have changed religions. In effect, my friends assumed I was writing a book on *evangelization*. They imagined that I was going to outline how conversions are to take place or that I would rehearse the necessity of living out the command of the Risen Jesus to "Go, therefore, and make disciples of all nations, baptizing them in the name of the Father, and of the Son, and of the holy Spirit . . ." (Matt 28:19).

Such reactions are not surprising, since even the dictionary emphasizes this aspect of conversion. *The American Heritage Dictionary* defines conversion as a "change in which one adopts a new religion."[3] This definition limits conversion to the individual experience of adopting a new religion, becoming a "born again Christian," or making converts by evangelizing the world through missionary activity. Little leeway is given to other descriptions of conversion. Henry J. Schmidt, writing on the limited understanding of conversion by many Christians, notes the difficulty of this narrow perspective: "A highly personalized, individualized, privatized version of Christianity that reflects individual transformation but fails to impact social relationships, societal structures and corporate lifestyle writes its own obituary in one word—irrelevance" (1980: vii).

A similarly narrow view of conversion underlies the common assumption of many Christians that they understand the biblical teaching of conversion. It boils down to a singular experience of being born again in Jesus Christ. It entails simply becoming a Christian and being saved on a given occasion. This may be due to overfamiliarity with only a few passages on conversion in the Bible. We do not always hold the Bible in proper perspective. Samuel Clemens (Mark Twain), the great American author, once wrote perceptively about this problem in a letter to a friend:

> People pretend that the Bible means the same to them at 50 that it did at all former milestones in their journey. I wonder how they can lie so. It comes of practice, no doubt. They would not say that of Dickens's or Scott's books. *Nothing* remains the same. When a man goes back to look at the house of his childhood, it has always *shrunk:* there is no instance of such a house being as the picture in memory and imagination calls for. Shrunk how? Why to its correct dimensions: the house hasn't altered, this is the first time it has been in focus[4] (his emphases).

What Clemens is getting at here is the difficulty of the loss of perspective. Once one has gained the perspective of distance, to take a new look at a familiar reality, then the real process of education begins. Twain goes on to note that this process requires a "loss" but also has its compensations. Though it means sacrificing an idealized view of the past, the new perspective allows one for the first time to have something in proper focus.

In my view, many Christians have the notion of conversion out of focus. The concept is either quite blurry, or it is so narrowly restricted that all perspective of the broader notion is lost in a hazy background. For so many of us, the biblical view of conversion is reduced to a once-for-all-time-born-again experience directed outwardly to the "heathen." It is usually "other people" who need to heed the message. It is seldom directed inwardly to ourselves and even less to a call to societal or ecclesial change.

An illustration of this attitude can be found in the experience of a pastor of a Catholic parish who recently wanted to conduct an adult education program titled, "We Are All Converts." The entire adult education committee was upset at the thought of such a title. They viewed themselves as "cradle Catholics," hardly the kind of people to be described as converts, let alone as people in need of a deeper conversion.

Many of us are so stuck on a broken record of calling other people to repent and believe in the good news that we have forgotten how the biblical message is directed to ourselves. This book aims to put the biblical teaching on conversion "in focus." If the problem of conversion is a blurred picture or too narrow a view of it, then a major aim of this book is to widen our NT horizons and finely tune our picture of conversion. The book strives to let the Bible speak for itself without the overlays of later preconceptions and misconceptions. It seeks to open our eyes to what we may have known but forgotten, to what we once experienced but what has since faded in memory. In short, it desires to provide a new vision of an old theme. This is a task worthy of conversion itself.

Types of Conversion

Above I mentioned that the NT evinces a fairly uniform understanding of conversion. This is not to say that all conversions are the same. Earlier studies have also noted that the NT contains evidence of at least three different *types* of human religious conversion. A solid study by Beverly Roberts Gaventa (1986), in particular, calls attention to "three categories of personal change" which are found in the NT: alternation, conversion, and transformation. She notes that the distinctions are not mutually exclusive, yet are distinctive enough for the following separate descriptions:

> Alternation is a relatively limited form of change that develops from one's previous behavior; conversion is a radical change in which past affiliations are rejected for some new commitment and identity; transformation is also a radical change, but one in which an altered perception reinterprets both past and present (1986: 12).

One must note that the common denominator in all three categories is *change*. All conversion involves a change. It is opposed to maintaining the status quo. Conversion always involves movement from one dimension to another. One might be tempted to see in these three categories merely evidence of a degree of conversion, but Gaventa rightly describes both conversion and transformation as "radical change," though their relationship between past and present is different. Instead, it is better to consider the three categories *aspects* of conversion found in the NT. Gaventa points to the story of the Ethiopian eunuch (Acts 8:26-39) as an example of alternation, and Paul (Acts 9; 22; and 26) as an example of conversion (1986: 148-49). She points to Paul's own self-description in his letters as evidence of transformation. But all of these cases are models of true conversion, the dramatic change which God's power has wrought in people's lives.

A modern theological and psychological approach to conversion, of course, will not be satisfied with such limited categories. Some prefer to examine conversion according to various dimensions of human transformation, such as religious, intellectual, moral, affective, and socio-political dimensions.[5] Others attempt more broadly to categorize conversions according to typologies: intellectual, mystical, experimental, affectional, revivalist, and coercive conversions.[6] However one tries to delineate distinctions in the human reality of conversion from psychological, theological, or sociological perspectives, the biblical data does not lend itself to such precision. This is partly due to the fact that biblical anthropology is more limited in scope than a modern view. The

Bible emphasizes the unity of the human person rather than distinct categories of human existence. Even the Greek distinction of body and soul, so essential to later Christian thought, is not the basis for the Hebraic anthropology of the Bible. Rather, the human person is viewed as an animated body, a unified whole. Thus, when the Bible speaks of conversion it involves the whole person and not merely one's moral sense, intellectual capacity, or spiritual life. Body, mind, and soul together are affected by the action of conversion, and implications are felt in all aspects of one's life, including the social and political arenas. For our purposes, then, the rather simple categories which Gaventa has outlined are sufficient background to delineate differences in the nature of conversion. For further theological or psychological dimensions, one should consult other studies which go beyond the biblical data.[7]

As we set off on an exploration of the NT understanding of conversion, I am reminded of an observation which Flannery O'Connor, the great Catholic fiction writer, is reported to have said about the importance of conversion. She asserted that conversion was "the only real subject of good literature."[8] That may be why she received so much inspiration from the Bible for her own works of fiction. If her criterion for measuring "good literature" is in any way valid, then the NT, as we shall see, surely qualifies, because it has much to teach us about conversion.

1

The Language of Conversion

The NT understanding of conversion did not develop in a vacuum. Just as all literature is influenced by its surrounding historical and cultural environment, so also the NT developed within a particular environment which imparted its own distinctive influences. One of the most important influences was, of course, the OT. Any exploration of the NT concept of conversion must first examine how the OT helped to shape it.

Old Testament Background

The OT notion of conversion is primarily expressed by two verbs, *nḥm* ("to regret" or "be sorry") and *shûb,* ("to turn, return, repent"). Both verbs are used transitively or intransitively, and the subject can be individuals, a group of people (e.g., Israel), or even God. The verb *nḥm* is used seldom if ever in the sense of repentance from sin. Indeed, it is rarely employed of human repentance and most frequently refers to God's reversal of intention. The word is not used of God's repentance from sin, since the OT does not conceive of God as a being who can commit sin.

Shûb is the more important word theologically (Holladay 1958) because it is most often used in the technical sense of human repentance or turning away from sin. It is curious, though, that the Septuagint (hereafter, LXX), the Greek translation of the OT, never translates *shûb* with the Greek word *metanoeō,* the word which in the NT is the technical word for conversion or repentance. Instead, the common Greek word to translate *shûb* is *epistrephō* ("to turn, return, turn back") or one of its cognates. Use of this word emphasizes the physical action of turning or returning rather than a change of mind or heart. But, of course, conversion has many metaphorical dimensions. How does the OT understand the concept of conversion?

There are two primary meanings to *shûb*. The first represents a physical turning and encompasses both turning *from* and turning *to* something or someone. Thus, one can return to a point of departure (Gen 14:7; 37:29), turn back in retreat (Ps 44:11), or return property (1 Kgs 20:34). But the second meaning has a deeper, more spiritual and theological sense. This is the sense which expresses most clearly conversion, a change of heart or an attitudinal redirection. Although the word *shûb* is found in every book of the OT except Haggai, this more profound second meaning tends to appear in the prophetic literature.[9] The reason for this is that the word applies primarily to covenantal contexts, especially the Mosaic covenant.[10] God's covenant with Moses entailed obligations on the part of the people (Exod 19:5–6; 20:1–17). The prophets became the chief voices calling the people back to these moral obligations. To see how varied the concept of conversion in the OT is, we will look at a few key passages.

A passage in the prophet Joel, often used by Christians on Ash Wednesday to begin Lent, is characteristic of the OT calls to conversion:

> [12]Yet even now, says the LORD,
>   return to me with your whole heart,
>   with fasting, and weeping, and mourning;
> [13]Rend your hearts, not your garments,
>   and return to the LORD, your God.
>   For gracious and merciful is he,
>   slow to anger, rich in kindness,
>   and relenting in punishment (Joel 2:12-13).

This text shows that the call to return to God is a strong exhortation to effect a dramatic turnabout in life. It is to be a redirection toward God, accompanied by visible symbolic actions, but rooted more profoundly in a fundamental, internal change of heart. At the center of the motivation for such a substantial change is recognition of the need for turning from evil and returning to a deep trust in the mercy of God.

Of the prophets none deserves to be called "king of the notion of conversion" more than Jeremiah. This is the label one scholar, E. K. Dietrich, has given him (Cazelles 1989: 26). A text which expresses profoundly the multiple senses of the OT concept of conversion is Jeremiah 8:4–6. The poetic alliteration of *sh* and *v* sounds unfortunately is lost in translation, but I will place the key Hebrew words in italics to show their varied meaning. God speaks to Jeremiah:

> ⁴Tell them: Thus says the Lord:
> When someone falls, does he not rise again?
>   if he goes astray (*yashûb*) does he not turn back (*yashûb*)?
> ⁵Why do these people rebel (*shôbʿbah*)
>   with obstinate resistance (*meshubah*)?
> Why do they cling to deceptive idols,
>   refuse to turn back (*lashûb*)?
> ⁶I listen closely:
>   they speak what is not true;
> No one repents (*niham*) of his wickedness,
>   saying, "What have I done!"
> Everyone keeps on running his own course,
>   like a steed dashing into battle.

This text illustrates well that both Hebrew verbs (*shûb* and *nhm*) can imply true conversion, turning back to God.[11] The breadth of expression of *shûb,* however, is astonishing. It encompasses turning away and turning back, rebellion and obstinate resistance. It is likened to one who stumbles and rises again, and to a horse rushing obliviously headlong into battle. One in need of conversion is a person who is obstinately going in one direction when he or she is in need of a one-hundred-eighty-degree turn!

The prophets frequently call for the people of Israel to turn especially from all forms of idolatry, as in the Book of Ezekiel:

> Therefore say to the house of Israel: Thus says the Lord God:
> Return and be converted from your idols; turn yourselves away
> from all your abominations (Ezek 14:6).

Hosea, too, issues the call to conversion and ties it to the forgiveness and healing of God which will follow:

> ²Return, O Israel, to the LORD, your God;
>   you have collapsed through your guilt.
> ³Take with you words,
>   and return to the LORD;
> Say to him, "Forgive all iniquity,
>   and receive what is good, that we may render
>   as offerings the bullocks from our stalls.
> . . .⁵I will heal their defection,
>   I will love them freely;
>   for my wrath is turned away from them (Hos 14:2-3, 5).

Isaiah is another prophet who calls for conversion, but he also adds a note of judgment which can be the consequence of not heeding the call:

> ¹⁸Come now, let us set things right,
>   says the LORD:
> Though your sins be like scarlet,
>   they may become white as snow;
> Though they be crimson red,
>   they may become white as wool.
> ¹⁹If you are willing, and obey,
>   you shall eat the good things of the land;
> ²⁰But if you refuse and resist,
>   the sword shall consume you:
>   for the mouth of the LORD has spoken!
>   (Isa 1:18–20; cf. also Ezek 18:30).

Jeremiah employs another image when he relates conversion to judgment. Through a chiastic parallel (seen in the words in italics/small capitals) he connects the human call to conversion with God's own action toward people who repent:

> ⁷Sometimes I threaten to *uproot* and TEAR DOWN and destroy a nation or a kingdom. ⁸But if that nation which I have threatened turns from its evil, I also repent of the evil which I threatened to do.

> ⁹Sometimes, again, I promise to BUILD UP and *plant* a nation or a kingdom. ¹⁰But if that nation does what is evil in my eyes, refusing to obey my voice, I repent of the good with which I promised to bless it (Jer 18:7-10).

This passage recalls Jeremiah's own call where his ministry as a prophet is described in the parallel tasks of uprooting and tearing down, building up and planting (Jer 1:10). From his perspective, the people of Israel are always in need of conversion because they are always turning away from the stipulations of the covenant. Like a garden that needs constant attention, like a building that needs continual repairs to keep it in good condition, so the people need a constant reminder to turn back to God.

We should note that this particular passage points to another aspect of conversion in the OT that is quite striking. It speaks of God "repenting" of or changing plans. In fact, elsewhere Jeremiah shows that God will cause a positive resolution of the image he has invoked because of a change of heart:

> If you remain quietly in this land I will *build you up,* and *not tear you down;* I will *plant you, not uproot you;* for I regret the evil I have done you (Jer 42:10).

Does God actually have regrets? Does God really change plans? In what sense is God the subject of conversion?

Actually there are numerous passages in the OT where God is spoken of as having a change of heart, most using the verb *nḥm* (Simian-Yofre 1986: 369-76), as we pointed out above. The notion is already present not long after the story of creation:

> ⁵When the LORD saw how great was man's wickedness on earth, and how no desire that his heart conceived was ever anything but evil, ⁶he regretted that he had made man on the earth, and his heart was grieved (Gen 6:5-6).

Later in Israel's history God is said to regret having made Saul the king (1 Sam 15:35). Moses, the great intercessor between God and the people of Israel, at times directly implores God to relent of the plans of destruction, as after the incident of the golden calf. Moses pleads, "Let your blazing wrath die down; relent in punishing your people" (Exod 32:12). And Moses gets results:

"So the LORD relented in the punishment he had threatened to inflict on his people" (Exod 32:14).

A more humorous treatment of God's ability to change plans, though not employing the technical language we have seen thus far, is found in Genesis. It is the story of Abraham bargaining with God over the destruction of the evil city of Sodom (Gen 18:20–32). This text portrays Abraham diplomatically bargaining with God by increments of five or ten:

> ²⁴"'Suppose there were fifty innocent people in the city; would you wipe out the place, rather than spare it for the sake of the fifty innocent people within it? ²⁵Far be it from you to do such a thing, to make the innocent die with the guilty, so that the innocent and the guilty would be treated alike! Should not the judge of all the world act with justice?" (Gen 18:24–25).

Abraham persists to forty-five, then forty, then more boldly to thirty and twenty, until at last he proposes merely ten innocent people! And God agrees that even if only ten can be found, the city will not be destroyed (v. 32). Abraham's bargaining works, and God relents. But, of course, there is also another side of this issue. If at times God is said to have "repented" of various intentions (usually judgment, as in Amos 7:3, 6), there are times when God is portrayed as unchanging and unrelenting (Jer 4:28).

Is all of this to be considered mere anthropomorphic projection of basic human emotions onto God, or is there a deeper meaning to such passages? With such texts we must avoid the modern tendency to philosophize and instead try to understand the biblical message on its own terms. While there are inevitably elements of anthropomorphism in ancient biblical texts, I believe the basic teaching is sound—God, too, is a being of change.

Terence Fretheim, an OT scholar, has explored the concept of the repentance of God (1988). He points to this metaphor as one among many images of God widely used in various OT traditions. Thus, "[d]ivine repentance . . . stands alongside some of the most fundamental statements Israel ever makes about its God. . .; it is believed to be just as characteristic of God as grace and mercy" (1988: 58). Fretheim goes on to point out the implication of this metaphor for God: ". . .it reflects the extent to which this loving and gracious God will go in order to execute God's uncompromising salvific actions'' (61). From the OT perspective, then, God is a God of change and of integrity, one who can set limits on relating to the world and yet who can also have a change of heart when deemed appropriate.

The OT certainly portrays God as one who can be affected by human pleas. The basis for prayers of petition is that our inner-most desires and needs will be heard by God and answered according to God's will. In fact, the penitential psalms speak of such expectation in the context of conversion. The greatest example is Psalm 51, attributed to David after his sin with Bathsheba. It is perhaps the most eloquent expression of contrition in the Bible:[12]

> [3]Have mercy on me, God, in your goodness;
>   in your abundant compassion blot out my offense.
> [4]Wash away all my guilt;
>   from my sin cleanse me.
> [5]For I know my offense;
>   my sin is always before me. . . (Ps 51:3–5).

Some scholars have looked for the source of the OT notion of conversion in the very origin of the people of Israel. They have proposed a ''revolt model'' of disparate, lower class individuals who ''converted'' to the Mosaic covenant with Yahweh and thus formed a people.[13] While this may or may not be the case, I think that a more likely source of an understanding of conversion comes precisely from the OT view of Yahweh as a God whose attitudes can change when people, too, have a change of heart. The Book of Jonah expresses it well in the story of the Ninevites who are called to repent:

> [9]''Who knows, God may relent and forgive, and withhold his blazing wrath, so that we shall not perish.'' [10]When God saw by their actions how they turned from their evil way, he repented of the evil that he had threatened to do to them; he did not carry it out'' (Jonah 3:9–10).

Does it seem ludicrous to think that God's ''conversion'' (in a metaphorical sense) could be related to our conversion (in an ethical sense)? I doubt that one could propose a better model of behavior.[14] What better model to follow in repentance than God?

If God can have a change of heart, then surely it is within our grasp as well. Christians find it essential to imitate Jesus (e.g., John 13:15), does it not follow *a fortiori* we could imitate God as well?

In any case, the OT is clear that God is the source of true conversion. It is not something which human beings themselves can accomplish. Even Jeremiah, who is very pessimistic about Israel's ability to effect conversion in any lasting fashion, sounds a hopeful note about God's action toward people in the context of conversion. Jeremiah records how God will change the situation by means of a new covenant (31:31–34), not by human ability or strength but by divine initiative (note the repetitive pronoun "I"):

> ³¹The days are coming, says the LORD, when *I* will make a new covenant with the house of Israel and the house of Judah. . . .³³*I* will place my law within them, and write it upon their hearts; *I* will be their God and they shall be my people (Jer 31:31, 33b; cf. 24:7).

In the NT this hope is explicitly tied to fulfillment in Jesus Christ (Luke 22:20; Heb 8:7–13).

A final aspect of conversion in the OT is that it is sometimes associated with symbolic gestures or rituals. The most prominent one, and the one which relates to the NT, is the use of water as ritual cleansing. The prophet Ezekiel, in particular, associates water with the renewal which will take place when God establishes a final effective covenant. The language evokes the new covenant language of Jeremiah which we just examined:

> ²⁵I will sprinkle clean *water* upon you to *cleanse* you from all your impurities, and from all your idols I will *cleanse* you. ²⁶I will give you a *new heart* and place a *new spirit* within you, taking from your bodies your stony hearts and giving you natural hearts. ²⁷I will put *my spirit* within you and make you live by my statutes, careful to observe my decrees. ²⁸You shall live in the land I gave your fathers; you shall be my people, and I will be your God (Ezek 36:25–28).

This passage constitutes Ezekiel's description of a spiritual heart transplant. That it is preceded by ritual cleansing is not unique.

Jewish life entailed a certain number of water rituals (e.g., the mention in John 2:6). Other parts of the OT employ water imagery as symbolic purification (e.g., Ps 51:4, 9; Zech 13:1). Other Jewish literature of the intertestamental period shows a similar development, for example, the Sibylline Oracles:

> Ah, wretched mortals, *change* these things, and do not lead the great God to all sorts of anger, but abandon daggers and groanings, murders and outrages, and *wash* your whole bodies in perennial *rivers*. Stretch out your hands to heaven and *ask forgiveness* for your previous deeds and make propitiation for bitter impiety with words of praise; God will grant *repentance* and will not destroy. He will stop his wrath again if you all practice honorable piety *in your hearts* (SybOr 4.162–70).[15]

Ritual baths also played a role in the life of the Essene community of Qumran. They were also for purposes of purification, and at least one passage places such cleansing in the context of a person who refuses to obey the terms of God's covenant properly and needs a behavioral change:

> For it is through a spirit of true counsel with regard to the ways of man that all his iniquities shall be wiped out so that he may look on the light of life. It is through a holy spirit uniting him to his truth that he shall be *purified* from all his iniquities. It is through the spirit of uprightness and humility that his *sin* shall be wiped out. And it is through the submission of his soul to all the statutes of God that his flesh shall be purified, by being *sprinkled with waters for purification and made holy by waters for cleansing* (I QS III.6b–9a).[16]

The language of this text is surprisingly reminiscent of NT imagery which we will examine in later chapters. It is sufficient to note here that the cleansing from sin and conversion to God's covenant are acts accompanied both by symbolic gestures and behavioral change. Interior conversion is mirrored in external behavior.

Summary

We have thus far laid out numerous threads of the OT tapestry of conversion. It is now time to weave them together into a coherent picture. We can summarize the OT understanding of conversion in ten major ways.

1) Philologically, though the basic meaning of conversion is *turning away* from evil and *turning to* God, we saw that more than one word is used to express conversion, and thus there are limits to what we gain from a study focused only on technical vocabulary.

2) A corollary to the above is that the OT speaks of conversion in a *panoply of images, expressions, and metaphors* that involve both God and human beings. Conversion is a reality that cannot be described by technical terms alone. Images of hearts being rent, plants being replanted, buildings being rebuilt, red turning white, and so on are part of the wide spectrum of expressions for this complex reality.

3) Conversion entails more than an outward expression of turning to God. It is a deeply *internal change* which involves the whole human person, a turning to God with whole heart, mind, and soul. It is thus both an act of reason and an act of will.

4) The OT emphasizes that conversion takes place in the context of *relationship*. The covenant is at the root of conversion, a relationship between God and human beings that exists because God desires it. This relationship comes with obligations. Any breech in fulfilling the obligations severs the relationship or severely damages it so that the unfaithful party must be "called back" to the relationship and its terms.

5) Conversion is also a *collective* event in the OT. The Psalms sometimes express ideas about conversion with the singular "I" but normally that represents the "typical I," the typical human being in need crying out to God (Löffler 1975: 30). The normal expression of conversion is, however, that an entire people return. God calls people into a relationship with God, a relationship that also has implications for living with other human beings. But individuals are not called to conversion alone.

6) Because conversion is a "call" to turn around or return, the OT clearly emphasizes that *God* is the one who initiates it: "Return, rebellious children, and I will cure you of your rebelling"

(Jer 3:22). True, there are mediators, like Moses or the prophets, to serve as mouthpieces for God's word, but God is the one issuing the call. As with any call, it requires a response to be effective.

7) Although humans alone need conversion from sin, God in the OT is said also to be a being of "conversion" in a metaphorical sense. Thus, God serves as a *model* of conversion in interrelationships with people.

8) It may be surprising to some, but the OT message of conversion is addressed *internally* to the people of God and not *externally* to others. That is to say, conversion is not a missionary activity of getting "converts" to a religion. The Israelites themselves are the ones who are called to conversion, to come back to the full stature of relationship with their God. This means that conversion is not turning to something totally new but *re*turning to what was formerly known.

9) Conversion is depicted not as a singular event but an *ongoing process* of realignment to God. God continually reaches out to human beings in relationship, yet we continue to stray from that relationship. Through conversion we make frequent course corrections in order to embrace the relationship to God anew.

10) Finally, conversion is an act accompanied by *symbolic gestures,* such as water rituals, and concrete changes in ethical behavior. Both reflect an internal change of heart.

We have thus seen that the "language" of conversion in the OT is broad and colorful. It contains many aspects which provide essential background for our exploration of the NT concept. We can now turn to an initial description of conversion in the NT through an examination of its language of conversion.

The Language of the New Testament

Every Christian probably recognizes that the basic NT word for conversion is the Greek word *metanoia,* meaning a change of mind, a change of direction, or an act of repentance. The verbal form, *metanoeō,* means to change one's mind, repent, be converted, or to feel remorse. Sometimes the noun is taken over into English as people describe their conversions as "metanoias." It is surprising, however, how seldom this word is used in the Gospels with the precise meaning of conversion. The Gospel of John does not even mention it once in either the verbal or nominal form. The statistics for the other Gospels are also relatively sparse. Mark, for instance, uses the noun *metanoia* only once and the verb twice. The noun appears in a passage which describes the ministry of John the Baptist as "proclaiming a baptism of repentance (*metanoia*) for the forgiveness of sins" (1:4). The specific connection between conversion and the forgiveness of sins which this passage shows appears elsewhere, especially in the Gospel of Luke, which uses the noun five times and the verb nine times. Between the frequency of usage exhibited by Mark and Luke lies that of the Gospel of Matthew. Matthew uses the noun only twice but employs the verbal form five times. Matthew's use of the vocabulary follows Mark at times, but there are also distinctive passages in Matthew where this terminology appears. We will look at specific passages in each Gospel in later chapters, but the point at present is to understand the meaning of the vocabulary of conversion in general.

Scholars have agreed upon the basic meaning of *metanoia* and *metanoeō* when used in the context of conversions. As in the OT, the main meaning has to do with a turning toward God, a substantive change in one's life. Whenever the nominal form of the word is used (twenty-two times in the NT), it is always in the singular rather than plural form. This usage emphasizes conversion as a process rather than a once-for-all-time action. The verbal form is frequently found in imperatival contexts, illustrating the exhortation to conversion.[17]

This notion relates to another Greek word the Gospels sometimes use with the same basic sense, *epistrephō*. We saw above that this was the word the Septuagint used to translate the Hebrew *shûb*. This word, which also has as its root meaning "turn" or "turn around," is used in connection with conversion only once in each of the Gospels. Three of these occurrences are actually parallel quotes from the same passage of the OT, Isaiah 6:10, where God gives the prophet Isaiah the difficult task of proclaiming a message to a stubborn Israel:

> You are to make the heart of this people sluggish,
>   to dull their ears and close their eyes;

Else their eyes will see, their ears hear,
their heart understand,
and they will turn (*epistrepsōsin*) and be healed.

(cf. Matt 13:15; Mark 4:12; John 12:40)

Each of the three Gospels quotes a slightly different version of this passage from Isaiah and uses it in a unique way. The original context of the passage in Isaiah is as part of the call narrative when the prophet receives his commission from God. These words which he is to speak to Israel foretell the obstinacy of the people that awaits the prophet when he preaches the strong and unwanted message of conversion. They will close their eyes and ears to God's call. Mark and Matthew show Jesus quoting this passage with respect to the failure of those outside the kingdom of God, i.e., those who reject Jesus and his teaching, who fail to comprehend the meaning of his parables. John, on the other hand, connects this passage with the failure of the crowds to believe in Jesus by virtue of the "signs" he has performed in his public ministry (John 12:37–38). In either case, a negative image predominates. The need for conversion is present but not accomplished. The failure to turn to God (in the case of Isaiah) or to Jesus (in the case of the Gospels) brings a divine judgment upon those involved.

The one Gospel instance of using *epistrephō* apart from the Isaian quote is a positive connotation found in Luke 22:31–32, the prediction of Simon Peter's denial. At the Last Supper Jesus says:

[31]"Simon, Simon, behold Satan has demanded to sift all of you like wheat, [32]but I have prayed that your faith may not fail; and once you have turned back (*epistrepsas*), you must strengthen your brothers."

Here Jesus seems to connect a "turning back" with a restoration of faith. This passage foreshadows Peter's later dominant role in supporting and leading the other apostles. Peter's "re-turn" from the repugnant denial of his master allows him to become, as Luke later tells the story in Acts, a major figure in the birth of the early church.

From this general perspective, then, what do we learn about the fundamental notion of conversion in the NT with regard to vocabulary? As in the OT, the root idea is clearly a turning. There is always movement in conversion. There is no room for the status quo, for lack of change. Conversion always involves a turning, whether a turning *from* something or someone or *to* something or someone. Although the NT employs the same basic vocabulary as the OT, there is a preference for using *metanoeō* and its cognates in a technical sense for conversion. But it is also surprising how seldom the NT actually speaks of conversion as changing one's mind or heart. The general NT sense of conversion is turning *(epistrephō)*. It involves turning away from sin, evil, or godlessness and turning toward God, Jesus, and a righteous life. But each section of the NT has a unique way of portraying the nature of Christian conversion.

Now that we have dealt with the basic linguistic data, the task of the rest of this book is to explore more thoroughly the diverse imagery used in the NT to describe conversion. Despite the lack of frequent occurrence of typical conversion language, we will see that the NT has a very broad understanding of this concept and that it is indeed central to Christian living. To begin our exploration, we will turn first to conversion according to the Gospel of Mark, which is generally considered to be the oldest of the Gospels.

2

Conversion in Mark: Following Jesus

Mark's Gospel begins with remarkable speed. Without any preparation the reader is thrust into the preaching of John the Baptist: "John [the] Baptist appeared in the desert proclaiming a baptism of repentance for the forgiveness of sins" (1:4). John's mission is to call people back to radical obedience to God's will, to get them to acknowledge their sinfulness and turn back to life in accord with God's laws. Although his ministry of conversion meets with some success, as seen in the numbers of people who go to the Jordan river for his baptism ritual (1:5), Mark makes it clear that John's ministry is merely preliminary to a greater call to conversion.

Jesus' Baptism: A Conversion?

The first specific action which occurs in Mark's Gospel is the baptism of Jesus (1:9–11). Mark's version of this story is brief and pointed.

> 9It happened in those days that Jesus came from Nazareth of Galilee and *was baptized* in the Jordan by John. 10On coming up out of the water he saw the heavens being torn open and the Spirit, like a dove, descending upon him. 11And a voice came from the heavens, "You are my beloved Son; with you I am well pleased."

Mark's straightforward account masks the consternation which the early Christian church felt over the fact of Jesus' baptism. To be frank, it was an embarrassment which had to be explained. Matthew's version (3:13–17) gives us a little hint of the controversy when he describes a conversation which takes place between John the Baptist and Jesus over who should be baptizing whom. Jesus permits John to proceed with the baptism: "Allow it now, for thus it is fitting for us to fulfill all righteousness" (Matt 3:15). Luke's Gospel (3:21–22), too, lessens the import of the actual baptism by placing the reference in a dependent clause described by a Greek participle in the passive voice—as indirect a way of referring to it as possible.

The crux of the matter is that in the early church baptism was automatically connected with forgiveness of sin, and yet christological beliefs about Jesus could in no way allow for his own need to be baptized by John. Like us, Jesus was viewed as having "similarly been tested in every way, yet *without sin*" (Heb 4:15; cf. John 8:46; 1 Pet 2:22; 1 John 3:5). So the problem was how to understand Jesus' baptism.

A few scholars wish to maintain that Jesus himself did indeed undergo a conversion experience.[18] It would be comforting perhaps to think that Jesus underwent a conversion just as we his followers are asked to undergo. It would make the modelling behavior of Jesus very overt. But the question needs to be raised: is Jesus' baptism as described in the NT evidence of a "conversion"? While no one would insist that it is a conversion in the sense of turning from sin, still one must make sense out of Jesus' baptism in order to understand his ministry. Mark, as the oldest Gospel, is a good place to examine the issue briefly.

The language Mark employs in describing Jesus' baptism, in my opinion, does not lead to a designation of conversion. Rather it is a private revelation of the *unique* relationship which Jesus had with God as that of a son to a father, a view confirmed by Jesus' usage of the Aramaic expression, *'abba'* (14:36) to address God as his father. Absent from the text is any kind of precondition necessary for conversion, whether it is a state of sinfulness or merely some incompleteness in life. No explanation is offered for Jesus' reception of baptism. Instead it is described as a private revelation from God, a dual visionary and auditory experience in which God reveals his divine paternity to Jesus. It is neither a conversion nor specifically a call,[19] but a unique christological revelation which characterizes Jesus' special status as God's Son and the eschatological harbinger of God's kingdom. Through an amalgam of OT texts (Ps 2:7; Isa 42:1; Gen 22:2) Jesus is revealed as the anointed one, the messiah, who is to bring a *message* of God's kingdom and the necessity of conversion to the world (1:15). This is not to deny that Jesus grew in self-understanding of his mission, but it indicates that with Jesus the category of conversion does not fit the evidence.

Jesus' Message of Conversion

At the beginning of his Gospel, then, Mark presents God's unique message to the world. He summarizes the beginning of Jesus' ministry succinctly:

> [14]After John had been arrested, Jesus came to Galilee proclaiming the gospel of God: [15]"This is the time of fulfillment. The kingdom of God is at hand. Repent, and believe in the gospel" (1:14–15).

For Mark, Jesus' sacred work can begin only after John is off the scene. Indeed, where John's message of conversion is expressed by the noun *metanoia* and is tied to baptism by water, the message of Jesus is expressed by the verb *metanoeō* and is superior to John's message because it entails a baptism "with the holy Spirit" (1:8). Jesus' message is made more urgent by this verbal idea; there is no time left, a radical change in life is needed now because it is the time of fulfillment. Jesus' message is sharply tinged with apocalyptic and eschatological urgency. The time is short; judgment is near, so action must be taken quickly. The tense of the verb (present imperative) may also communicate the message that conversion is an ongoing process.[20] Conversion will always mark the life of a disciple.

Jesus connects his urgent command to "repent" with an equally urgent call to *"believe in the gospel."* Mark's understanding of conversion is intimately connected with faith. The word "gospel" here does not mean a written Gospel as is found in the NT, but the total message of conversion and salvation which Jesus came to bring, that is, the "good news." For Mark, believing in this good news cannot be separated from faith in Jesus himself.

This brings us to the central teaching of Mark's Gospel about conversion. Christian conversion means to follow Jesus, i.e., to become a disciple and to have faith in Jesus. In fact, the first act which Jesus performs after proclaiming his central message is to call his first disciples together (1:16-20). This action sets up the thematic thrust of the rest of the Gospel. It is basically a story of faith and discipleship.

Faith and Discipleship

But Mark's understanding of conversion is not summarized only in the two passages we have seen above. The verb *metanoeō* is used one more time in Mark, in the context of Jesus' own ministry. Mark 6:7-13 describes Jesus sending out his own twelve specially chosen disciples to share in his ministry. In addition to giving them a share in the power to heal and cast out demons, Jesus sends the disciples out to preach a message: "So they went off and preached repentance" (6:12; literally: "that people should repent"). The disciples' ability to share in Jesus' call to conversion does not reduce their own need to hear the same message, for indeed, the lion's share of Mark's Gospel is devoted to both the challenge and failure of discipleship. In this way Mark's understanding of conversion goes beyond the use of standard vocabulary for it.[21]

Once the first disciples are called, Jesus sets out in earnest accomplishing the deeds which verify John the Baptist's prediction that a mightier one would come (1:7). Jesus casts out demons (1:21-26), heals the sick (1:32-34; 2:1-12), and gets into disputes with Jewish leaders over his authority and ability to do the things he does (2:18-22). He even cures Simon's own mother-in-law (1:29-31). As his select chosen ones witness these events, they are also instructed in the secrets of God's kingdom which are revealed in Jesus (the parable chapter, 4:1-34). As Mark's story of Jesus and the disciples develops, one would expect that the disciples would fulfill Jesus' expectations and become the loyal followers he invites them to be. What a surprise to find out along the way that this expectation goes largely unfulfilled!

Fear, Incomprehension, and Faith

Biblical scholars have often noted that Mark tends to show the disciples of Jesus in an unfavorable light. Despite all of the marvels which they witness in the ministry of Jesus, they are often described as bumbling, thick-headed people who just don't seem to understand. They are like the occasional characters of the comic strip, "Mister Boffo," who are described as "people unclear on the concept." Jesus often has to ask them in these or similar words: "Are even you likewise without understanding?" (7:18).

The disciples are contrasted with other characters in the story. Even demons recognize Jesus and what he represents, as Mark 3:11 shows: "And whenever unclean spirits saw him they would fall down before him and shout, 'You are the Son of God' '' (cf. 1:24, 34). Yet the disciples seem oblivious to this recognition. Even after Jesus has explained the parables to them in chapter four, they demonstrate their incomprehension. At the conclusion of this chapter, in the story of Jesus calming the storm at sea (4:35–41), their true lack of faith and understanding, coupled with their fear, bubbles to the surface. After they plead with Jesus in cowardly fashion to save them from the angry sea, Jesus can only ask: "Why are you terrified? Do you not yet have faith?" (4:40). And the disciples are left puzzling, "Who then is this whom even wind and sea obey?" (4:41).

Discipleship and Blindness

Nowhere is this motif of fear and lack of understanding clearer than in the central section of Mark which is almost exclusively devoted to the teaching of true discipleship. This great section stretches from 8:22, the story of the blind man at Bethsaida, to 10:52, the conclusion of the story of blind Bartimaeus. Indeed, this technique of framing passages on discipleship with the "bookend" stories of two blind men helps to get the point across with irony. These blind figures "see" by means of Jesus who is just passing by, while the disciples remain "blind" to the Jesus who is always with them!

Mark weaves throughout this section of the Gospel teachings about Jesus' identity as the Son of Man who must suffer, and the challenge of the disciples to follow after him. The three main pillars around which Mark weaves his themes are the passion predictions (8:31–33; 9:30–32; 10:32–34). These are alternated with glimpses of the glory that is hidden in Jesus' identity, namely, Peter's confession of Jesus as the Messiah (8:27–30) and the transfiguration (9:2–8). But in the midst of these revelations there remains a consistent resistance on the part of the disciples to comprehend fully the meaning of Jesus' teachings, actions, and identity. Though Jesus instructs them explicitly on the conditions of discipleship (8:34–38), that it is necessary to lose one's life in order to gain it, the disciples end up disputing over who should get the best place at the eternal banquet (10:35–41). Lest the Gospel reader mistakenly think the message is meant only for the disciples who star in Mark's story, the account of the rich man who tries to follow Jesus on his own terms warns otherwise (10:17–22). Unknown outsiders who want to follow Jesus also have a tough time effecting such a major change in their lives. How hard it is to be a disciple! How hard it is singularly to be undistracted by wealth, power, prestige, or influence to concentrate solely on following Jesus. But this is just what conversion from Mark's perspective requires.

At the conclusion of this section of the Gospel, the unremitting blindness of the disciples is contrasted with the true sight of Bartimaeus. Once Jesus tells Bartimaeus that his faith has saved him, Mark records his response: "Immediately he received his sight and followed him on the way" (10:52). This willingness to follow Jesus is made all the more poignant by the fact that the next scene begins the larger narrative of the passion of Jesus with the triumphal entry into Jerusalem (11:1–11). On the path that leads to suffering and death, the disciples will show themselves to be the cowardly, fearful ones that they are; they will betray, deny, and desert their own master. But a "blind" man will follow Jesus, nonetheless.[22]

Conversion and Discipleship

Some want to read Mark's story in such a way that the disciples are, then, irredeemable figures, lost in their inability to make a firm commitment to Jesus and overwhelmed by the fear that paralyzes them into inaction.[23] But this is not Mark's intention. Rather, Mark uses the disciples to provoke in his reading/hearing audience the insight that discipleship is extremely difficult.[24] It is not easy to follow Jesus. It is not easy to apply the message of conversion to oneself. If anyone is looking for an easy way to be a disciple, Mark's Gospel will not provide the means for that self-disillusionment. On the contrary, the point for Mark is that discipleship is risky business. The big opponent of faith is not harboring *doubts* but holding onto *fear*.

Mark's Jesus can never be understood apart from the necessity to endure the cross, or, more importantly, to embrace it. To use the famous expression of Dietrich Bonhoeffer, the Lutheran pastor killed by the Nazis in World War II, there is no such thing as "cheap grace" for Mark. There is a "cost of discipleship." Mark's Jesus is deadly serious when he says, "Whoever wishes to come after me must deny himself, take up his cross, and follow me" (8:34). Mark will have none of the facile talk of being "born again" as if it is some fantasy-like, miraculous event which suddenly makes the whole world seem rosy. Mark offers no way to sweep our failures away and pretend they were never there.

If Mark does not often speak of language familiar to conversion as we know it, it is not because it is tangential to Jesus' message as Mark presents it. On the contrary, conversion is central to the message of Jesus. In some ways, it is *the* central notion of the Gospel because embracing the kingdom of God requires repentance from sin and faith in Jesus. But Mark describes it entirely in terms of discipleship and faith. Conversion means recognizing that discipleship cannot be limited to preaching a message to others without applying it to oneself in equal share. Essentially, Mark seems to give a warning to all who would follow Jesus. Watch out! You, too, can fail to understand. You, too, can be afraid to change your heart, your attitudes, your very lives to follow a path that is rocky and strewn with pitfalls. Perhaps that is why the Gospel ends in such an ambiguous manner with the women at the empty tomb:

Then they went out and fled from the tomb, seized with trembling and bewilderment. They said nothing to anyone, for they were afraid (16:8).

Such ambivalence places the burden of understanding on the shoulders of the hearer/reader of the Gospel. The women are put precisely in the position of a decision. They can let fear prevent them from fulfilling the angel's command to announce the resurrection (16:6-7), or they can overcome their fear and proclaim the gospel boldly and courageously. Since the reader/hearer has received the story of Jesus from others, the second alternative must have won out, but Mark never narrates it. The choice for the women was no less difficult than for any other would-be disciple. And that choice places the challenge squarely before the reader/hearer who must choose as all the disciples have had to throughout Mark's story. You have to decide to follow Jesus once you have heard the call. You have to choose to overcome your fear in order to progress to the level of faith that embraces the cross and the suffering which it entails.

Mark's understanding of conversion is thus a very challenging one. It is described in terms of discipleship and faith. It is marked by the sign of the cross, and it is a message that applies to *all* disciples, regardless of rank or stature. Keeping Mark's understanding of conversion on these terms before us can prevent us from falling into the trap of quick conversions and easy grace. Following Jesus is not easy, and it never was. The poet, Robert Frost, expressed this sentiment well in a popular poem that emphasizes the power of difficult choices: "Two roads diverged in a wood, and I, I took the one less travelled by, and that has made all the difference." Mark's Gospel reminds us that conversion takes us down the more difficult road.

3

Conversion in Matthew:
Bearing Good Fruit

The Gospel of Matthew also connects conversion with discipleship but with greater complexity than Mark. Matthew agrees with Mark that conversion is at the heart of Jesus' message. He also makes explicit that both John the Baptist and Jesus called people to radical conversion in life. Their message is expressed with exactly the same words: "Repent (*metanoeite*), for the kingdom of heaven is at hand!" (Cf. 3:2 and 4:17).[25] But Matthew also gives conversion a particular ethical twist. To understand how this is so, we will analyze Matthew's understanding of conversion according to three major interrelated themes: bearing good fruit, the coming judgment, and the challenges of discipleship.

Bearing Good Fruit

The most prominent Matthean image of conversion is taken from the agricultural setting of Palestine. In a harsh desert land, possessing trees and plants that can yield a plentiful and healthy harvest is essential to survival. The OT itself speaks of fruitfulness of the land, plants, animals, and people, but occasionally it also uses the term "fruit" metaphorically for the results of people's actions (Prov 1:31; 11:30; Isa 3:10; Jer 32:19; Hos 10:13).

Matthew transforms this notion into an ethical concept about living the proper life according to God's will.[26]

The first mention of this theme is in the context of John the Baptist's preaching of conversion:

> [7]When he saw many of the Pharisees and Sadducees coming to his baptism, he said to them, "You brood of vipers! Who warned you to flee from the coming wrath? [8]Produce good fruit as evidence of your repentance (*poiēsate karpon axion tēs mctanoias*). [9]And do not presume to say to yourselves, 'We have Abraham as our father.' For I tell you, God can raise up children to Abraham from these stones. [10]Even now the ax lies at the root of the trees. Therefore every tree that does not bear good fruit will be cut down and thrown into the fire" (3:7–10).

The intimate connection with judgment, which we will discuss below, is apparent in this passage. But just as striking is the outright challenge to the Jewish leaders to give some evidence that they have changed their ways. The Greek expression literally reads, "bear fruit worthy of conversion," i.e., one's deeds in life should give ample evidence that they conform to the proper life God intends. There can be no reliance upon heredity, such as in the figure of the patriarch Abraham. Instead, one's own ethical behavior is the concrete example of whether or not one's life reflects God's will.

John's vigorous message is matched by that of Jesus near the conclusion of the Sermon on the Mount (5—7):

> [15]"Beware of false prophets, who come to you in sheep's clothing, but underneath are ravenous wolves. [16]By their fruits you will know them. Do people pick grapes from thornbushes, or figs from thistles? [17]Just so, every good tree bears good fruit, and a rotten tree bears bad fruit. [18]A good tree cannot bear bad fruit, nor can a rotten tree bear good fruit. [19]Every tree that does not bear good fruit will be cut down and thrown into the fire. [20]So by their fruits you will know them" (7:15–20).

In this case, the image of bearing fruit is not directed to opponents of Jesus who need to be converted but to disciples. Jesus warns the community that there exist false prophets (cf. 10:41 and

23:34) who would lead them astray. But, just as the saying goes, "the proof is in the pudding," so the community of disciples is warned that the deeds of these people will be the evidence of their true intentions. The passage is framed by the repeated line: "by their fruits you will know them." Again the ethical intent comes to the fore. It is inconsistent that good people will do bad deeds and vice versa. Matthew places emphasis on concrete evidence that people are living life properly in accordance with God's design. From his perspective, people reap exactly what they sow.

The same metaphor is employed in the context of the Pharisees' opposition to Jesus' action of driving out a wicked demon (12:22–32). They accuse him of being in cahoots with Satan himself, to which Jesus responds that a divided kingdom cannot survive. He extends the image employing the metaphor of fruit:

> [33]"Either declare the tree good and its fruit is good, or declare the tree rotten and its fruit is rotten, for a tree is known by its fruit. [34]You brood of vipers, how can you say good things when you are evil? For from the fullness of the heart the mouth speaks. [35]A good person brings forth good out of a store of goodness, but an evil person brings forth evil out of a store of evil. [36]I tell you, on the day of judgment people will render an account for every careless word they speak. [37]By your words you will be acquitted, and by your words you will be condemned" (12:33–37).

Jesus reinforces the earlier message more explicitly, that as trees are known by their fruit so people are known by their deeds, but he offers a further insight. It is not just *deeds* that matter, but *words* as well can reveal the true nature of a person, because words reflect an interior attitude that issues from the heart. We must keep in mind, of course, the biblical understanding of the heart. Unlike our modern understanding of the heart as the center of love, the biblical view is that it is the locus of moral, rational, and volitional conduct.

This insight is particularly appropriate to Matthew's perspective. Matthew has a great concern that interior motivation be matched by exterior reality. In place of attention to the external mechanics of religiosity, Matthew's Jesus insists on a proper interior attitude. When he and his disciples are criticized for not adhering to religious traditions such as washing the hands (15:1–20), Jesus quotes Isaiah's lament that "this people honors me with their lips, but their hearts are far from me" (Isa 29:13 LXX). He goes on to apply the message further:

> [11]"It is not what enters one's mouth that defiles that person; but what comes out of the mouth is what defiles one. [18]. . .But the things that come out of the mouth come from the heart, and they defile. [19]For from the heart come evil thoughts, murder, adultery, unchastity, theft, false witness, blasphemy. [20]These are what defile a person, but to eat with unwashed hands does not defile" (15:11, 18–20).

Even in the context of this passage the agricultural image reappears: "Every plant that my heavenly Father has not planted will be uprooted" (15:13). This statement appears here as a reminder of Matthew's perspective. Although the ethical demands of conversion are strong, Matthew has no illusions about what can make the efficacy of these demands a reality in the Christian community. It is God's own grace that causes the miraculous productivity of the kingdom. The parables of Jesus, many of which are concerned about plants and growth, make this clear for Matthew (13:1–53).

The parable chapter contains a series of related images that reinforce and expand the notion of bearing fruit as a primary metaphor for conversion. The parable of the sower (13:1–8) shows how some seed falls on rich soil and produces a magnificent, if uneven, harvest. It is explicitly interpreted to show the fecundity of God's word in the person of one who receives it: "But the seed sown on rich soil is the one who hears the word and understands it, who indeed bears fruit and yields a hundred or sixty or thirtyfold" (13:23). The parable of the weeds among the wheat (13:24–30) shows that wicked people and good people often are mixed together, but at the great eschatological harvest they will be separated out, as is made clear in the interpretation of this parable (13:36–43). Two smaller parables emphasize the miraculous growth of God's kingdom. The kingdom is compared to a tiny mustard seed that grows into a huge sheltering tree (13:31–32) and to yeast that makes a whole batch of dough rise (13:33). In both instances, it is God's mysterious grace that brings fruition.

The importance of bearing fruit in life comes to the fore in two other instances by way of negative example. Immediately after the scene of the cleansing of the temple (21:12–17) comes the brief passage of the cursing of the fig tree (21:18–22):

> [18]When he was going back to the city in the morning, he was hungry. [19]Seeing a fig tree by the road, he went over to it, but found nothing on it except leaves. And he said to it, "May no fruit ever come from you again." And immediately the fig tree withered (21:18–19).

At first glance, this seems like a whimsical action, as if Jesus had gotten up on the wrong side of the bed and is taking it out on the poor fig tree! But in Matthew's perspective, the cursing of the fig for its lack of fruit is nothing less than a prophetic sign of Israel's failure to effect a true conversion (cf. 3:10). It thus becomes symbolic of the judgment which will come upon Jerusalem and all Israel for the failure to heed the word of God and put it into practice.

The same negative perspective is even more apparent in the Matthean version of the parable of the wicked tenants (21:33–43).[27] This time Jesus employs the image of a vineyard (a common image for Israel in the OT, e.g., Isa 5:1–7):

> [33]"There was a landowner who planted a vineyard, put a hedge around it, dug a wine press in it, and built a tower. Then he leased it to tenants and went on a journey. [34]When vintage time (*ho kairos tōn karpōn*) drew near, he sent his servants to the tenants to obtain his *produce* (*tous karpous autou*). [35]But the tenants seized the servants and one they beat, another they killed, and a third they stoned. [36]Again he sent other servants, more numerous than the first ones, but they treated them the same way. [37]Finally, he sent his son to them, thinking, 'They will respect my son.' [38]But when the tenants saw the son, they said to one another, 'This is the heir. Come let us kill him and acquire his inheritance.' [39]They seized him, threw him out of the vineyard, and killed him. [40]What will the owner of the vineyard do to those tenants when he comes?" [41]They answered him, "He will put those wretched men to a wretched death and lease

his vineyard to other tenants who will give him the *produce* at the proper times" (*tous karpous en tois kairois autōn*). ⁴²Jesus said to them, "Did you never read in the scriptures:

> 'The stone that the builders rejected
> has become the cornerstone;
> by the Lord has this been done,
> and it is wonderful in our eyes'?

⁴³Therefore, I say to you, the kingdom of God will be taken away from you and given to a *people* that will produce its *fruit* (*ethnei poiounti tous karpous autēs*)" (21.33–43).

This passage can appropriately be considered the climax of the theme of conversion as "bearing fruit" in Matthew's Gospel. That the call to the conversion of Israel has failed is self-evident in this parable. As a virtual allegory of salvation history, the attempts of the vineyard owner (= God) to gain the fruit of the vineyard at harvest time (*kairos*) are thwarted by the abusive treatment of his servants (= prophets) and outrageous death of his own son (= Jesus, the rejected stone). When Jesus asks the opinion of the Jewish leaders²⁸ how the vineyard owner will respond, they fall into the trap of ironically stating their own condemnation in a forceful manner. Those "wretched" ones will receive a "wretched" end, and the vineyard (= kingdom) will be given to better tenants who will give over the fruit at harvest time. That is precisely the judgment which issues from Jesus' mouth in verse 43! It is significant that the word *ethnos* (Greek, "nation" or "Gentile") is used, for doing so makes the judgment crystal clear: Israel as a people has failed to produce the fruits of the kingdom, so another people (i.e., those who follow Jesus, many of whom will be Gentiles) will be given the chance to effect a proper harvest. The use of *kairos* is also significant here. Although it represents the time of harvest (cf. 13:30), it is also a word which means a time of fateful decision, a propitious time to act (cf. 26:18). Conversion is just such a time. The interplay of bearing fruit at harvest time with *ethnos* packs this parable with a punch. From Matthew's perspective, Israel's failure to heed the message of conversion, its inability to bear proper fruit, leads to a forfeiture of the privileges of the kingdom.

The Coming Judgment

Closely allied to the notion of "bearing fruit" is that of the coming apocalyptic judgment which the kingdom will inaugurate (Michiels 1965: 62–63). This is an element of Matthew's Gospel with which, I suspect, many contemporaries will be uncomfortable. We find judgment a hard pill to swallow. We live in an era that stresses the power of positive thinking and the need to be non-judgmental of people. How does the role of judgment in conversion fit the message of Jesus as "good news"?

Matthew cannot separate judgment from conversion. We have seen this in passages quoted above. It is part and parcel of the strict oppositions that abound in Matthew's Gospel. Just as trees that do not bear good fruit will be thrown into the fire (3:10; 7:19) or weeds are gathered up only to be burned (13:30), so will those who do not heed the call to conversion be doomed to a condemnation of "wailing and grinding of teeth" (a favorite Matthean expression of judgment; see 8:12; 13:42, 50; 22:13; 24:51; 25:30). The conclusion of the Sermon on the Mount lays out the two choices one has:

> ²⁴"Everyone who listens to these words of mine and acts on them will be like a wise man who built his house on rock. ²⁵The rain fell, the floods came, and the winds blew and buffeted the house. But it did not collapse; it had been set solidly on rock. ²⁶And everyone who listens to these words of mine but does not act on them will be like the fool who built his house on sand. ²⁷The rain fell, the floods came, and the winds blew and buffeted the house. And it collapsed and was completely ruined" (7:24–27).

This passage is truly foundational (pun fully intended!) for Matthew's perspective because of its key position at the conclusion of the Sermon and because of its content. Matthew emphasizes that people have choices when they consider following Jesus. He believes that those who make good choices build firm foundations and can withstand the vicissitudes of life, but those who make bad choices risk utter folly.

The Matthean understanding of judgment reaches its apex in the final great discourse of Jesus concerning the eschatological trials and tribulations (24—25). Jesus recites a series of parables with contrasting figures which make it clear that the coming kingdom is one that will entail a strict judgment between those who were prepared and those who were not. The first contrasting example is between the faithful servant who is rewarded for his vigilant care of the master's household, and the unfaithful servant who squandered his time away and is punished upon the master's sudden return (24:45-51). A second example is the contrast between the five wise virgins who awaited the bridegroom with extra oil in their lamps, and the five foolish virgins who were caught unprepared (25:1-13). The foolish virgins find themselves locked out of the wedding feast! A third example is the lengthy parable of the talents (25:14-30). Pity the poor wretched servant who hid the one talent his master gave rather than risk investing it. Not only is he punished by being thrown into the darkness, but his talent is given away to the one with the most. The final example is the famous parable of the sheep and the goats (25:31-46) in which the "goats" go off to eternal punishment while the "sheep" (the righteous) go off to eternal life.[29]

All of these scenes of future judgment are tinged with eschatological tension. They are ominous warnings about the future if we do not choose wisely. Yet, to emphasize judgment from a negative perspective, as if Jesus were a finger-wagging parent warning wayward children, "you'd better watch out," is to miss the point. The function of these passages about judgment is broader in scope. They serve to provoke people to choose discipleship more directly, on the one hand, yet on the other hand they also offer a message of hope for those who have left all to follow Jesus (19:27-30). The deeper message of the judgment passages is that there is coming a kingdom which will reverse the apparent fortunes amassed on earth. Jesus set forth this vision in the Beatitudes (5:3-12). The poor in spirit and those persecuted for righteousness will inherit the kingdom; the meek will inherit the earth; mourners will be comforted; and so on. Indeed, in the coming kingdom the faithful ones will "shine like the sun" (13:43) and their reward will be great (5:12; 10:41-42). The message of judgment, then, from a disciple's perspective is a promise of future reward, a time when all wrongs will be righted, when the first and last will exchange places (19:30; 20:16).[30]

The Challenges of Discipleship

A third way in which Matthew gives conversion an ethical twist is in the description of the challenges of discipleship. Matthew makes it clear that conversion is a process of change, of turning from one way of life to another. Jesus instructs the disciples:

> [3]"Amen, I say to you, unless you turn (*straphēte*) and become like children, you will not enter the kingdom of heaven. [4]Whoever humbles himself like this child is the greatest in the kingdom of heaven" (18:3–4).

A disciple's life is a life of humility,[31] characterized by the law of boundless love (5:43–48; cf. 22:34–40), a willingness to serve others rather than be served (20:25–28), and an ability to forgive innumerable times (18:21–35).

The Matthean ethical demands of discipleship are many and complex, but three noteworthy aspects stand out. The first is the importance of doing the "will of God." Matthew portrays Jesus as God's faithful and obedient Son, who both knows the will of his father and accomplishes it.[32] But doing God's will is also at the heart of discipleship. A key phrase in the "Our Father" instructs the disciples to pray in earnest, "your will be done" (6:10; cf. Jesus' own prayer in Gethsemane, 26:42), and the mark of a true family member is not blood relationship, but doing the will of God (12:46–50). Confessing Jesus' identity alone is insufficient for salvation, one's life must conform to God's will:

> "Not everyone who says to me 'Lord, Lord,' will enter the kingdom of heaven, but only the one who does the will of my Father in heaven" (7:21).

A second aspect of the ethical demands of discipleship is that Jesus calls his followers to the way of "greater righteousness" (Greek, *dikaiosynē*).[33] This Matthean theme is found especially in the Sermon on the Mount (5:6, 10, 20; 6:1, 33) and is thus directed to the disciples, but it is also characteristic of John the Baptist (21:32) and Jesus himself (3:15). Matthew does not create the notion of righteousness out of whole cloth. Rather he adopts a traditional OT understanding of righteousness as fulfilling the ethical demands which God places upon human beings. Matthew then exalts the importance of this concept as constitutive of discipleship.

One cautionary note is needed regarding the notion of righteousness. We must not understand Matthew's idea as related to *self-*righteousness. Although the disciples are called to live righteously, the call to discipleship is one of true conversion. Jesus explicitly states: "I did not come to call the righteous but sinners" (9:13). The disciples, then, are not pictured as perfect people. Indeed, one of Matthew's favorite expressions for them is "you of little faith" (6:30; 8:26; 14:31; 16:8). They have faith but not enough. They are then like ordinary would-be disciples: called to righteousness, but not yet there, called to perfection (5:48) but quite imperfect, called to avoid sin, yet remaining sinners. In this fashion, disciples for Matthew are always in need of conversion.

A third aspect of the demands of discipleship is single-hearted devotion. In the Sermon on the Mount the disciples are challenged to "seek first the kingdom [of God] and his righteousness, and then all these things will be given you besides" (6:33). Matthew sees Jesus' call to conversion as a radical call to a univocal, undivided way of life. Hypocrisy is condemned in no uncertain terms (e.g., 6:2, 5, 16; 15:7-9; 23:23-28). The root idea of hypocrisy (from the Greek, *hypokrisis*) stems from the masks which Greek actors wore on the stage. What Jesus calls disciples to is authentic human existence in accord with God's laws, not "wearing masks," i.e., playing roles or performing empty religious rituals. Disciples are to exhibit a proper inner attitude that is born out in good external behavior. Their lives are to be characterized by attention to the weightier matters of God's law, like justice, mercy, and faith, and not just to the mechanics of being a religious person (cf. 9:13; 12:7; 23:23). The giving of one's whole heart and mind and soul to God is nothing short of a radical conversion in human life, a total transformation. Jesus' challenge to the rich young man to forsake his belongings and follow him (19:16-24) demonstrates how difficult the message of Jesus really is, because there are so many distractions in life. But Jesus' explanation of this circumstance shows the path:

> ²⁵When the disciples heard this, they were greatly astonished and said, "Who then can be saved?" ²⁶Jesus looked at them

and said, "For human beings this is impossible, but for God all things are possible" (19:25-26).

Matthew lays out a difficult challenge for any disciple to respond to, but he gives the assurance that God's own power can provide the desired efficacy.

A Special Case of Conversion

Thus far we have examined Matthew's understanding of conversion from the perspective of the standard NT vocabulary and the way Matthew gives it his own ethical twist. But there is one other way in which Matthew speaks of conversion. Matthew is the only Gospel to employ the Greek word *metamellomai* ("change one's mind," "repent"). He does so three times in two separate passages (21:29, 32; 27:3). Most scholars judge this word as lacking the technical meaning of conversion which *metanoeō* or *epistrephō* have, but is this the case?[34] Let us examine briefly the two passages where the word occurs.

The first use of the word is in Jesus' parable of the two sons addressed to the Jewish leaders (21:23):

> [28]"What is your opinion? A man had two sons. He came to the first and said, 'Son, go out and work in the vineyard today.' [29]He said in reply, 'I will not,' but afterwards he changed his mind (*metameletheis*) and went. [30]The man came to the other son and gave the same order. He said in reply, 'Yes, sir,' but did not go. [31]Which of the two did his father's will?" They answered, "The first." Jesus said to them, "Amen, I say to you, tax collectors and prostitutes are entering the kingdom of God before you. [32]When John came to you in the way of righteousness, you did not believe him; but tax collectors and prostitutes did. Yet even when you saw that, you did not later change your minds (*metemelethete*) and believe in him (21:28-32).

I believe three strong factors support the contention that *metamellomai* in this passages stands for true conversion. (1) The use of two opposite figures, one a negative model and the other a positive one, reflects Matthew's tendency which we saw earlier to view reality in terms of the choice between two opposites. The son who changed his mind and did his father's "will" is precisely a good example of what true conversion is all about. (2) The vocabulary used in the parable fits neatly with the Matthean understanding of conversion we have examined thus far. In particular, mention of John the Baptist and the "way of righteousness," the failure on the part of the Jewish leaders to "believe," and the fact that notorious sinners like "tax collectors and prostitutes" are the ones who "believe," all relate to conversion. Sinners are the ones who respond to Jesus' call rather than the self-righteous. (3) The context itself supports the notion that this parable provides a true example (in negative and positive fashion) of conversion. It is both preceded and followed by two images of judgment against Israel because of the failure to heed Jesus' message of conversion, namely, the cursing of the fig tree (21:18–22), and the parable of the wicked tenants (21:33–43), both of which we examined above. The parable thus serves well as the third component of a trilogy on conversion.

The third occurrence of *metamellomai* is in the narration of the suicide of Judas Iscariot (27:3–10). The *Revised New Testament of the New American Bible,* which we have been using in this book, has the following translation of the key sentences:

> ³Then Judas, his betrayer, seeing that Jesus had been condemned, *deeply regretted* (*metamelētheis*) what he had done. He returned the thirty pieces of silver to the chief priests and elders, ⁴saying, "I have sinned in betraying innocent blood." They said, "What is that to us? Look to it yourself." ⁵Flinging the money into the temple, he departed and went off and hanged himself (27:3–5).

Other translations are similar, using expressions like "filled with remorse" (*NJB*) or "seized with remorse" (*REB*).[35] One can see by the phraseology that the editors of these translations do not think Judas "repented" of his action. Rather, they see it as psychological regret, but something short of true repentance or conversion. However, I believe this action can be viewed as a "conversion," albeit in an incomplete and flawed sense.

Three factors weigh in favor of viewing this as a true conversion rather than a mere change of mind. (1) Judas uses the expression "I have sinned" (*hēmarton*), the most common NT statement which indicates the beginning of the conversion process, the acknowledgement of sinfulness. (2) Judas also acknowledges by the expression "innocent blood" that his actions have led to an unjust condemnation of an innocent man. He thus admits the nature of his sin and recognizes its gravity. (3) His action of flinging the money back into the temple concretely illustrates his desire to dissociate himself from his prior despicable behavior. But to what purpose could this story be viewed as a conversion?

There is, of course, one missing element in this story of Judas' conversion. His suicide removes the possibility of receiving the loving forgiveness of his heavenly Father. But this missing element is precisely what makes of Judas a proper *negative example* of conversion for Matthew's readers/hearers. Judas, by taking the conversion into his own hands, fails to do the one other necessary prerequisite for a fully effective conversion. He fails to place his life completely into the hands of God. In this sense, though his perspective is one of true repentance for his sin, the larger perspective of the story indicates that his conversion was a failed attempt. In this fashion, Judas becomes a negative model of a conversion in Matthew.[36] This aspect challenges the reader/hearer of the Gospel to reexamine closely the nature of true conversion and its role in a disciple's life.

Summary

In this chapter we have seen how Matthew's understanding of conversion is more multi-faceted than Mark's. Matthew employs the same basic vocabulary of conversion, but takes it in a different direction. He makes it more of an ethical concept and ties it to a wealth of images surrounding discipleship: bearing good fruit, the coming judgment, and the challenges of discipleship. In typical fashion, Matthew has a penchant for viewing reality in mutually exclusive opposites. Thus, one is either good or evil, for or against Jesus (12:30), thinking the way God does or the way human beings do (16:23). Conversion is a matter of a choice with serious ramifications. It can lead to salvation, but failure to effect it leads to condemnation. Matthew thus uses both negative and positive examples to communicate his message. He also goes beyond the use of the technical vocabulary of conversion and employs another term (*metamellomai*). But at the heart of the concept conversion is still the basic understanding of turning away from sin and folly and turning to God.

4

Conversion in Luke: Prodigal
Children of a Prodigal God

Recent biblical scholarship has exhibited a good tendency to treat Luke-Acts together as the only two-volume work in the NT, properly recognizing their interrelationship.[37] While respecting this approach, I have chosen to treat the Gospel separately from Acts for two reasons. The first is that the Gospels, as a unique kind of literature, contain similar passages which, for the sake of comparison and contrast, are better treated in tandem. The second is that, while Acts and Luke definitely belong together and are written by the same author, a thematic study such as this requires precision in noting developments or changes of theme. Acts, in fact, shows significant thematic development and has an intense interest in conversion unparalleled in any other part of the NT. Consequently, it will be treated in a separate chapter.

Lukan Special Interest in Conversion

The Gospel of Luke shows more interest in the notion of conversion than Mark and Matthew combined (Lacan 1978a: 113). This would be evident alone by the fact that the primary words for conversion occur more frequently (*metanoia* five times, *metanoeō* nine times). Of the fourteen occurrences, ten are found in Lukan passages not common to Mark or Matthew, a clear indication of special interest. Moreover, Luke expands the understanding of conversion by connecting it more explicitly with other themes, especially forgiveness and reconciliation, salvation, the mercy of God, and joy. These themes help to diffuse the eschatological urgency of conversion found in Mark and Matthew's understanding while simultaneously increasing its personal dimension (Michiels 1965: 76).

That conversion is going to be central to Luke's Gospel is already clear in the infancy narrative. The birth of John the Baptist as precursor to Jesus is heralded by the double use of the word *epistrephō* at the onset of a new ministry of conversion:

> "He will be filled with the holy Spirit even from his mother's womb, ¹⁶and he will *turn* many of the children of Israel to the Lord their God. ¹⁷He will go before him in the spirit and power of Elijah to *turn* the hearts of fathers toward children and the disobedient to the understanding of the righteous, to prepare a people fit for the Lord" (1:15c-17).

John's ministry has two foci representing spiritual and social implications. He is to turn Israelites to God. But he is also to turn people to one another. Characteristic of Luke's interest in human reconciliation, John's call to conversion challenges fathers to act more justly to their children and disobedient people to come to know a more righteous life.

John's ministry of turning people back to God is confirmed by his father Zechariah's great canticle in response to John's birth. In it Zechariah heralds John's ministry of conversion by explicit reference to salvation and forgiveness of sin:

> ⁷⁶And you, child, will be called the prophet
> of the Most High,
> for you will go before the Lord
> to prepare his ways,
> ⁷⁷to give his people knowledge of salvation
> through the forgiveness of their sins. . . (1:76–77).

This special Lukan connection of conversion with forgiveness of sin is echoed in John's own preaching "a baptism of repentance for the forgiveness of sins" (3:3)[38] and his challenge to the Jewish leaders to "produce good fruits as evidence of your repentance" (3:8).[39]

Luke's infancy narrative also lays out the pattern of conversion as the result of God's action toward people. God not only sends special messengers (John and Jesus) to mediate salvation, but the entire story of Jesus and the church is guided by God's Holy Spirit.[40] Conversion springs from the action of God's mercy extended to people in the form of salvation. Mary's song of praise hails God "whose mercy is from age to age" (1:50), who remembers mercy according to the covenantal promises (1:54-55), and who acts toward people with great and tender mercy (1:58, 78).[41] God brings salvation in fulfillment of the ancient prophetic promises of the Old Testament (1:69-70), a salvation which has not only a spiritual dimension but includes "salvation from our enemies and from the hand of all who hate us. . ." (1:71). The actual designation of "savior" is applied to both God (1:47) and to Jesus (2:11), the only such explicit designations in the Synoptic Gospels.[42] When Jesus is mocked at the crucifixion, it is in terms of his saving action toward others. "He *saved* others, let him *save* himself if he is the chosen one, the Messiah of God" (23:35; cf. 23:37, 39). But Jesus continues to direct his saving actions toward others. Not only does he cry out, "Father, forgive them, they know not what they do" (23:34),[43] but when he is defended by the one repentant thief with whom he is crucified, he promises him salvation (23:40-43). The irony is that he who saves sinners by his blood (22:20) is himself condemned by sinners (24:7). The realities of conversion, salvation, and forgiveness are inextricably linked in Lukan theology.[44]

The emphasis on forgiveness of sins found in the ministry of John the Baptist also appears in the teaching of Jesus. Jesus explains his mission with the metaphor of a doctor and patients.

> "Those who are healthy do not need a physician, but the sick do. I have not come to call the righteous to repentance (*eis metanoian*) but sinners" (Luke 5:31b-32).

Luke's addition of the phrase *to repentance* (cf. Mark 2:17; Matt 9:13) makes explicit the connection between the call to conversion and the need for sinners to be healed of their sinfulness. The reconciliation and forgiveness of the Father is precisely the kind of medicine prescribed to heal this afflicted state.

The Contribution of Luke 15

Nowhere does Luke reveal his interest in conversion as reconciliation and forgiveness more than in chapter 15, in a series of parables, two of which are unique to this Gospel.[45] In response to the Pharisees' and scribes' complaint that he is hanging around with sinners (15:1–2; cf. 7:34, 37, 39; 19:7), Jesus tells the parable of the lost sheep:

> ⁴"'What man among you having a hundred sheep and losing one of them would not leave the ninety-nine in the desert and go after the lost one until he finds it? ⁵And when he does find it, he sets it on his shoulders with great joy ⁶and, upon his arrival home, he calls together his friends and neighbors and says to them, 'Rejoice with me because I have found my lost sheep.' ⁷I tell you, in just the same way there will be more joy in heaven over *one sinner who repents* than over ninety-nine righteous people who have no need of *repentance*" (15:4–7).

What is striking about this story is the drastic measure the shepherd takes to seek out *one* lost sheep. Ninety-nine are left in the desert in jeopardy so that the lost one can be brought back to the fold! Several other aspects of the story are important, too. The sheep did not stray (contrast Matt 18:12) but is "lost," and the shepherd takes the initiative to find it. Such is the sinner's condition prior to conversion, and God's response is to seek out the lost. Another aspect so prominent in Luke is the note of joy which accompanies such a successful repentance.[46] Rather than being a grudging act of change, repentance is touted as an action leading to great rejoicing. Such is the result of true conversion for Luke. It is the experience of being lost, then found, which leads to boundless joy.

Luke then records a parallel parable of the same motif, the parable of the lost coin, this time using a woman as the central figure:

8"'Or what woman having ten coins and losing one would not light a lamp and sweep the house, searching carefully until she finds it? 9And when she does find it, she calls together her friends and neighbors and says to them, 'Rejoice, with me because I have found the coin that I lost.' 10In just the same way, I tell you, there will be rejoicing among the angels of God *over one sinner who repents"* (15:8–10).

The motif of lost and found climaxes in the most remarkable parable of Luke's Gospel, the famous parable of the prodigal son (15:11–32). No other parable portrays more poignantly that God operates a lost and found department, and yet none of the typical vocabulary of conversion, repentance, or returning appears! Instead, Luke allows the power of the story itself to communicate its message:

"A man had two sons, 12and the younger son said to his father, 'Father, give me the share of your estate that should come to me.' So the father divided the property between them. 13After a few days, the younger son collected all his belongings and set off to a distant country where he squandered his inheritance on a life of dissipation. 14When he had freely spent everything, a severe famine struck that country, and he found himself in dire need. 15So he hired himself out to one of the local citizens who sent him to his farm to tend the swine. 16And he longed to eat his fill of the pods on which the swine fed, but nobody gave him any. 17Coming to his senses he thought, 'How many of my father's hired workers have more than enough food to eat, but here am I, dying from hunger. 18I shall get up and go to my father and I shall say to him, "Father, I have sinned against heaven and against you. 19I no longer deserve to be called your son; treat me as you would treat one of your hired workers."' 20So he got up and went back to his father. While he was still a long way off, his father caught sight of him and was filled with compassion. He ran to his son, embraced him and kissed him. 21His son said to him, 'Father, I have sinned against heaven and against you; I no longer deserve to be called your son.' 22But his father ordered his servants, 'Quickly bring the finest robe and put it on him; put a ring on his finger and sandals on his feet. 23Take the fattened calf and slaughter it. Then let us celebrate with a feast, ²⁴because this son of mine was dead, and has come back to life again; he was lost, and has been found.' Then the celebration began" (15:11–24).

Up to this point in the parable the most remarkable aspect is the extravagance of the father's love toward his son. Not only does he give him his inheritance before his time and let him go off on his own, but then he welcomes him back with open arms and rewards his return despite his son's extravagant profligacy. The father's hyperbolic language upon the son's return betrays the "prodigal" nature of his love. In place of the expected normal sequence of being lost and found, dead and alive, the father reverses it and says, "this son of mine was dead, and has come back to life again; he was lost, and has been found." Conversion is not only being refound when lost but actually coming to life again after death, a potent signal of the promise that Jesus came to bring (24:6–7). The text conveys this *divine* prodigal love shown by the father even further, as the voice of *human* reason (in the figure of the elder son) comes to play:

> ²⁵"Now the older son had been out in the field and, on his way back, as he neared the house, he heard the sound of music and dancing. ²⁶He called one of the servants and asked what this might mean. ²⁷The servant said to him, 'Your brother has returned and your father has slaughtered the fattened calf because he has him back safe and sound.' ²⁸He became angry, and when he refused to enter the house, his father came out and pleaded with him. ²⁹He said to his father in reply, 'Look, all these years I served you and not once did I disobey your orders; yet you never gave me even a young goat to feast on with my friends. ³⁰But when your son returns who swallowed up your property with prostitutes, for him you slaughter the fattened calf.' ³¹He said to him, 'My son, you are here with me always; everything I have is yours. ³²But now we must celebrate and rejoice, because your brother was dead and has come back to life again; he was lost and has been found' " (15:25–32).

If we were honest with ourselves, we would probably acknowledge sympathy with the elder son. After all, he has been faithful and obedient the whole time, while the younger son has been irresponsible in the extreme. The story can easily offend our sense of justice. But our sense of justice forgets God's mercy. Nowhere does the story intimate that the father has any less affection for the elder son just because he is overjoyed at the return of his younger son. There is enough love in the father to go around, but the older son wants it restricted only to those who *deserve* it. And therein lies the rub! The younger son does not deserve to be treated this way, but Luke's Jesus says that this is exactly how sinners are treated who decide to come back, to admit their failing, to humble themselves to start anew, and to rejoin the Father of all. Only those who are not self-righteous but who humble themselves like the tax collector, and who cry out, "O God, be merciful to me a sinner" (18:13; cf. 5:8), will experience true conversion. The force of this conversion is that the dead come to life, the lost are found, and this leads to a great rejoicing. In one well-told tale, Luke describes the essence of conversion to perfection without ever using the technical word for it.

Zacchaeus and Conversion

This complex of themes surrounding conversion (lost/found; salvation to sinners; joy) comes together in another uniquely Lukan passage about the diminutive tax collector, Zacchaeus (19:1–10). In an effort to see Jesus as he passes through Jericho, Zacchaeus climbs a tree. The story continues with Jesus' actions:

> ⁵When he reached the place, Jesus looked up and said to him, "Zacchaeus, come down quickly for today I must stay at your house." ⁶And he came down quickly and received him with *joy*. ⁷When they all saw this, they began to grumble, saying, "He has gone to stay at the house of a *sinner.*" ⁸But Zacchaeus stood there and said to the Lord, "Behold, half of my possessions, Lord, I shall give to the poor, and if I have extorted anything from anyone I shall repay it four times over." ⁹And Jesus said to him, "Today *salvation* has come to this house because this man too is a descendant of Abraham. ¹⁰For the Son of Man came to *seek* and to *save* what was *lost*" (19:5–10).

Jesus, who has often demonstrated the power to forgive sins (cf. 5:17-26; 7:47-50), again takes the initiative and offers salvation to a despised tax collector. It is another example of God's gracious action toward sinners, but it is equally important to see Zacchaeus's own actions. Jesus brings salvation but Zacchaeus receives Jesus joyfully and also demonstrates his personal change of life by generous almsgiving and by repaying extravagantly any fraud. Ironically, the one who was seeking Jesus found himself the object of God's own search for one in need of conversion.

We have found thus far that Luke emphasizes the joyful aspect of conversion, especially compared to Matthew. Are there no negative aspects to consider? We need to investigate this matter further.

A Sterner Notion of Conversion?

In another uniquely Lukan parable, the tone of his understanding of conversion shifts somewhat. Jesus describes for his disciples the parable of the rich man and Lazarus (16:19-31). In the midst of a favorite Lukan theme about the rich and the poor, a mention of conversion reveals another aspect of Luke's understanding. The poor man Lazarus dies and goes to Abraham's bosom while the rich man (never named, but traditionally known as "Dives") goes to the netherworld. Because of the torment of the netherworld the rich man wants Lazarus to fetch him some water to relieve his thirst. But, when he is told a chasm separates the two places, he asks that Lazarus be allowed to go back to the world to warn his five brothers, lest they end up in the same predicament. Abraham then responds:

> "They have Moses and the prophets. Let them listen to them."
> [30]He [the rich man] said, "Oh no, father Abraham, but if someone from the dead goes to them, they will *repent.*" [31]Then Abraham said, "If they will not listen to Moses and the prophets, neither will they be persuaded if someone should rise from the dead" (16:29-31).

At first glance this story appears to offer a threat if one does not repent, but other factors indicate that the emphasis lies elsewhere.

First, Abraham's words indicate that the *means* of hearing the message of conversion are already within the grasp of those who desire it. The mention of Moses, the figure most connected with the law, along with the prophets, is a clear reference to the scriptures of the Old Testament. Those who would really heed the message of conversion are referred to the scriptures. In them is sufficient teaching to bring about a true change of mind and heart in those who seek the kingdom.

A second aspect is the mention of the resurrection. Luke here intimates that even after Jesus rises from the dead, the most remarkable confirmation that he was God's ultimate eschatological messenger, the message of conversion will not be heeded. This foreshadows the difficult time the gospel will have being accepted by everyone who hears, but does not overshadow its success. Luke develops this story in his second volume, Acts, which describes the spread of the gospel throughout the world accompanied by periodic opposition and persecution.

The end of Luke's Gospel provides a clear indication that conversion from sin is an essential part of the message to be carried to the world. The Risen Jesus gives his disciples final instructions immediately prior to his ascension:

> "Thus it is written that the Messiah would suffer and rise from the dead on the third day ⁴⁷and that *repentance, for the forgiveness of sins,* would be preached to all the nations, beginning from Jerusalem. ⁴⁸You are witnesses of these things. ⁴⁹And [behold] I am sending the promise of my Father upon you; but stay in the city until you are clothed with power from on high" (24:46–49).

The phrase, "repentance, for the forgiveness of sins," functions in both a backward looking and forward looking fashion. From a retrospective vantage point it brings the ministry of John the Baptist, who preached the same message (3:3), full circle. Prospectively, it looks to an essential part of the preaching of the apostles in Acts. For example, when Peter and the apostles are brought before the Sanhedrin and questioned about their activities, they respond:

> "We must obey God rather than men. ³⁰The God of our ances-
> tors raised Jesus, though you had him killed by hanging him
> on a tree. ³¹God exalted him at his right hand as leader and
> savior to grant Israel *repentance and forgiveness of sins.* ³²We
> are witnesses of these things, as is the holy Spirit that God has
> given to those who obey him" (Acts 5:29–32).

The message is, as Luke foreshadowed, not well received by the
Jews (cf.the negative reaction in Acts 5:33). Yet it shows the in-
separable connection between conversion and forgiveness of sins,
which is a hallmark of the Lukan perspective. This is a reflection
of the teaching of Jesus himself in a passage which juxtaposes
both primary verbs for conversion with the verb "forgive."

> If your brother sins, rebuke him; and if he repents (*metano-
> ēsē*), *forgive* him. And if he wrongs you seven times in one day
> and returns (*epistrepsē*) to you seven times saying, 'I am sorry,'
> (*metanoō*) you should *forgive* him (17:3–4).

From this passage arises again Luke's concern that conversion
has a horizontal dimension (human person to human person) as
well as a divine dimension (human to God). This is the same attitude expressed by the prayer Jesus gives his disciples: ". . .for-
give us our sins for we ourselves forgive everyone in debt to
us. . ." (11:4).

Thus far our exploration of the Lukan understanding of conversion has put great emphasis on the connection with forgiveness. One can rightly ask, are there no stern challenges and
warnings about conversion such as was more evident in Matthew?

Luke does have vestiges of a sterner view of conversion, but
they recede far into the background in comparison to Matthew.
For example, Luke also records the reproaches to the unrepen-
tant towns of Chorazin and Bethsaida (10:13–16; cf. Matt 10:15;
11:20–23) and the mention of the sign of Jonah as a sign of repentance which should be heeded (11:29–32; cf. Matt 12:38–42).
Luke's reference to Jonah brings a strong warning of judgment:

> At the judgment the men of Nineveh will arise with this gener-
> ation and condemn it, because at the preaching of Jonah they

repented, and there is something greater than Jonah here (11:32).

But in the sum of things, Luke's view of God's attitude toward conversion comes down much more on the side of mercy and forgiveness than on the side of threat and condemnation. When a person turns from sin and returns to God, Luke's view is that the heavens themselves will rejoice and the sinner will be welcomed back with open arms.

Luke contains another passage which might suggest a stern call to repentance coupled with a threat. But careful examination of it in context indicates that it fits neatly with our earlier description.

> ¹At that time some people who were present there told him [Jesus] about the Galileans whose blood Pilate had mingled with the blood of their sacrifices. ²He said to them in reply, "Do you think that because these Galileans suffered in this way they were greater sinners than all other Galileans? ³By no means! But I tell you, *if you do not repent,* you will all perish as they did! ⁴Or those eighteen people who were killed when the tower of Siloam fell on them—do you think they were more guilty than everyone else who lived in Jerusalem? ⁵By no means! But I tell you, *if you do not repent,* you will all perish as they did!" (13:1–5).

This uniquely Lukan passage would seem to contradict our portrayal of the Lukan teaching of conversion as a rather joyful act. It would seemingly emphasize that the lack of conversion entails the threat of sudden folly. Nothing is known outside of Luke of the two incidents used as an object lesson for conversion. Whether it concerns Pilate's renowned firebrand cruelty or an unfortunate construction accident, the message seems to be that, unless you change your life around in repentance, the same quick, unexpected end will await you! The double repetition of the conditional clause, "if you do not repent, you will all perish as they did," hardly sounds like the Luke we have seen so far, who seems willing to pronounce forgiveness at the slightest hint of turning around. But the wider context helps us see how Luke understands this passage. It is not meant to promote action out of guilt. Luke couples these examples with a parable:

⁶And he [Jesus] told them this parable: "There once was a person who had a fig tree planted in his orchard, and when he came in search of fruit on it but found none, ⁷he said to the gardener, 'For three years now I have come in search of fruit on this fig tree but have found none. [So] cut it down. Why should it exhaust the soil?' ⁸He said to him in reply, 'Sir, leave it for this year also, and I shall cultivate the ground around it and fertilize it; ⁹it may bear fruit in the future. If not you can cut it down' " (13:6–9).

Both Matthew (Matt 21:18–19) and Mark (Mark 11:12–14) employ the image of a fig tree as a symbol of the destruction which will come upon Jerusalem, but only Luke records this parable of the fig tree. Connected as it is with the firm call to repentance we saw above, we can see now how Luke wishes us to understand conversion in its deepest sense. The patience of the orchard owner to be persuaded to let the fig tree have one more year to produce fruit is like the patience of God with the sinner. You get one more chance! Unlike baseball, where it's three strikes and you're out (v. 7, "three years"!), Luke's God always leaves room for one more opportunity. This is not a watering down of the call to conversion. Luke is certainly serious that the readers of his Gospel (and Acts) seize the opportunity to repent. There *is* an ultimate sanction, even as the parable indicates (v. 9). But he emphasizes the infinite patience God has with sinners. This is surely good news for procrastinators and backsliders, which is what we all are as sinners in one fashion or another.

Summary

This brief exposition of the Lukan notion of conversion needs to be enhanced yet by the development of the concept in Acts, but we can summarize our understanding thus far. Luke has the same basic starting point as Mark and Matthew, situating the call to conversion in the ministries of both John the Baptist and Jesus. But he quickly takes it in a different direction. By explicitly connecting conversion with the forgiveness of sins, Luke goes a long way to *personalizing* conversion. Rather than the broad call to the conversion of a people or a nation (as in the Old Testament)

Luke emphasizes the call to conversion which individuals must heed. Sinners must turn away from sin and come back to God. As soon as these prodigal children return, they will be met by a forgiving Father who will immediately rejoice at their return and celebrate with great festivity. The mercy of God, whose love seems itself prodigal, will not only know no bounds, but will be exercised with infinite patience. For Luke, conversion and repentance, forgiveness and reconciliation, are all part of the "wideness of God's mercy." In short, Luke's view of conversion as merciful reconciliation takes on a familiar appearance of conversion as we have experienced in the Church's understanding of the Sacrament of Reconciliation. Little wonder that many Lukan passages (especially the prodigal son) become the centerpiece for reconciliation services. For an even more familiar notion of conversion, we turn now to the Acts of the Apostles.

5

Conversion in Acts:
From Blindness to Sight

Probably the very mention of the Acts of the Apostles brings to the average Christian's mind the notion of conversion. Virtually everyone associates Acts with conversion because of the great conversion stories of Paul on the road to Damascus or the Ethiopian eunuch. With Acts we reach familiar territory, conversion viewed as changing religion or as seeking to convert pagans to Christianity. In many ways Acts is *the* book of conversion in the NT, but we need to examine passages carefully to see how Acts is both consistent with the rest of the NT in its understanding of conversion and nuances that understanding.

Acts uses the standard NT vocabulary for conversion (*metanoeō* and *epistrephō*) in a conventional fashion. It can make reference to the OT understanding of the Israelites turning from God (7:39; cf. 7:42) or can associate conversion with turning away from sin and turning back to God (Gaventa 1986: 41–43, 96), although it shows a preference for using *epistrephō* in conversion contexts (Hulsbosch 1966: 63). One of Peter's early speeches in Acts indicates this by reference to God's message of conversion directed to the Jewish people: "For you first, God raised up his servant and sent him to bless you by *turning* each of you from your evil ways" (3:26).[47] Gentiles, too, are urged to "turn from these idols to the living God" (14:15). In addition to the association with a turn from evil, Acts directly associates repentance with conversion by connecting both Greek verbs in the same breath. Peter's aforementioned speech contains an explicit exhortation: *"Repent, therefore, and be converted,* that your sins may be wiped away. . ."* (3:19), and this is consistent with Paul's own testimony recorded in a later speech: ". . .I preached the need to *repent* and *turn* to God, and to do works giving evidence of repentance"* (26:20). Repentance and conversion are thus two aspects of the same reality which involves turning from sin back to God.

If the vocabulary sounds familiar, nevertheless Acts nuances the concept of conversion in three ways. (1) In keeping with Luke's treatment of personalized conversion, but beyond the more communal call to conversion in Mark and Matthew, Acts *individualizes* it by focusing on individual stories of conversion. (2) Contrary to treating conversion primarily as a message directed *inwardly* toward the community of disciples, Acts directs conversion *outwardly* toward incorporating non-members into the Christian community. Outsiders are invited to join "the Way," a favorite Lukan self-designation for the new faith community (9:2; 19:9, 23; 22:4; 24:14, 22).[48] (3) A related concept is that, in comparison to the Synoptic Gospels, Acts frequently denotes conversion as an overt *change of religion,* specifically from paganism to Christianity. This may be one reason why Christians today often narrowly focus conversion to the task of making religious converts. These generalizations having been stated, we turn now to examine Acts more closely.

Jacques Dupont, in a classic study of conversion in Luke's second volume (1979: 61–62), states that three things are essential to conversion in Acts: a sense of sinfulness, a relationship to the resurrection of Jesus, and a dramatic change of life. Unlike the Synoptic Gospels, Acts does not emphasize that conversion is an eschatological act directly related to the kingdom of God (Hulsbosch 1966: 62). Rather, conversion is firmly attaching oneself to a faith community established through the resurrection of Jesus and sustained by the power of the Holy Spirit. Much of the teaching about conversion in Acts is contained in speeches which major characters in the narrative deliver on various occasions. Scholars have long recognized that these speeches, far from being a literal record of historical orations, are rather rhetorical vehicles for the evangelist to set forth his own ideas. Peter's speech immediately following the Pentecost event contains a mini-gospel summarizing the significance of the life, death, and resurrection of Jesus. In response to this speech comes a primary reference to conversion in Acts:

> [37]Now when they heard this, they were cut to the heart, and they asked Peter and the other apostles, "What are we to do, my brothers?" [38]Peter [said] to them, *"Repent* and be *baptized,* every one of you, in the name of Jesus Christ for the *forgiveness of your sins;* and you will receive the holy Spirit. [39]For the promise is made to you and to your children and to *all those who are far off,* whomever the Lord our God will call. . . .[41]Those who accepted his message were *baptized,* and about three thousand persons were added that day (2:37–39, 41).

This first mention of conversion in Acts is noteworthy for several reasons. First, although Peter's speech is directed to a *group* of people, it is *individuals* within the group who are called to respond to the exhortation to repentance. This is typical of Acts, which records how large groups of people are converted and yet which always emphasizes the importance of individual conversions.[49] Second, it is essential to see that, for Acts, conversion is always related to baptism. Baptism in the name of Jesus[50] is the appropriate response to the call of conversion, and it both wipes away sinfulness and incorporates one into the Christian community.

Third, even in this passage directed to the Jewish hearers (2:14), one gets a hint of the universal dimension of the call to conversion which is a hallmark of Luke-Acts. The reference to "those who are far off" is not a reference to the Jews of the diaspora but to the Gentiles (cf. 22:21). From Luke's perspective, the ones who will ultimately respond to God's call to conversion will be the Gentiles. This is made clear in many ways throughout Acts, but is nowhere more evident than at the conclusion of the book. While Paul is in captivity in Rome, he continues to appeal to the Jews to accept the gospel message. When he fails to get their concession, he quotes the same Isaian passage we have examined before (above, pp. 19–20):

"'Well did the holy Spirit speak to your ancestors through the prophet Isaiah, saying:
²⁶'Go to this people and say:
You shall indeed hear but not understand.
   You shall indeed look but never see.
²⁷Gross is the heart of this people;
   they will not hear with their ears;
      they have closed their eyes,
so they may not see with their eyes
   and hear with their ears
and understand with their heart and *be converted,*
   and I heal them.'
²⁸Let it be known to you that this *salvation* of God has been sent to the *Gentiles;* they will listen" (28:25b–28).

The explicit transference of the gift of God's salvation from the Jews to the Gentiles is a striking feature of the view of Luke-Acts. Luke uses this quote from Isaiah to justify the outreach to the Gentiles. The failure of Israel to heed the message of conversion, and the willingness of the Gentiles to do so, has grave consequences in the economy of salvation envisioned by Luke-Acts. On the one hand, the Jewish failure to respond to God's call is associated with ignorance (3:17; 13:27; cf. Luke 23:34), understood as a "deliberate failure to acknowledge the true God" (Dupont 1979: 64), and with putting Jesus to death (2:23; 3:14–15; 10:39; 13:28). On the other hand, the turning to the Gentiles is viewed as part of God's divine plan for the spread of the gospel "to the ends of the earth" (1:8). In fact, the two aspects are intimately tied together, as is clear in a passage about why Paul and Barnabas "turn" to the Gentiles:

⁴⁶Both Paul and Barnabas spoke out boldly and said, "It was necessary that the word of God be spoken to you [Jews] first, but since you reject it and condemn yourselves as unworthy of eternal life, we *turn* now to the Gentiles. ⁴⁷For so the Lord has commanded us, 'I have made you a light to the Gentiles, that you may be an instrument of salvation to the ends of the earth' " (13:46–47).

The "conversion of the Gentiles" (15:3) is both a cause for great joy to the Christian community and a problem. Luke's perspective is one which immediately raises the ticklish question about whether the NT is anti-Semitic. Although this would take us far afield, we must address the issue briefly with regard to the perspective of Luke-Acts.[51]

Is Luke-Acts Anti-Semitic?

Despite the uncompromisingly negative language of some passages in Acts which seem to condemn the Jews *en masse* for the death of Jesus, at least four factors militate against jumping to the conclusion that Luke-Acts is anti-Semitic. In the first place, it is anachronistic to speak of anti-Semitism in the NT. While we live in a post-Holocaust period of seeing the enormous injustice which has been perpetrated by Christians toward Jews through the ages, we cannot impose this understanding on the NT. We must always remember that NT debates, quarrels, and battles were often fought from the perspective of *intra-Jewish* discussions, which could frequently be quite intolerant and even violent.

Second, Luke-Acts views the death of Jesus not simply from a viewpoint of culpability. Rather, Jesus' death was in strict accordance with God's plan that it was "necessary" (Greek, *dei*, Luke 9:22; 17:25; 24:7, 26; cf. Acts 17:3) for Jesus to suffer, die and be raised. Even in places where some Jews are implicated in Jesus' death, Luke states strongly that it was part of God's plan: "This man, delivered up by the *set plan and foreknowledge of God,* you killed, using lawless men to crucify him" (2:23). The emphasis is not on culpability but on a divine plan of salvation.

A third factor to consider is that Acts clearly envisions the early Christian community as a mixture of Jews and Gentiles. The earliest members of the community are Jewish followers of Jesus, and one of the greatest heroes of Acts is Paul, the Jewish "convert," whose story we will consider shortly. Acts 15 even shows that the community could continue to observe Jewish legal regulations while allowing the Gentile converts greater freedom in that regard. Peter and James become spokesmen for such a position:

> [9]"He [God] made no distinction between us and them [Gentiles], for by faith he purified their hearts. [10]Why, then, are you now putting God to the test by placing on the shoulders of the dis-

ciples a yoke that neither our ancestors nor we have been able to bear?'' ''. . .[19]It is my judgment, therefore, that we ought to stop troubling the Gentiles who turn to God, [20]but tell them by letter to avoid pollution from idols, unlawful marriage, the meat of strangled animals, and blood'' (15:9–10; 19–20).

Jews and Gentiles existed side by side in the early Christian community, even if many Jews (and Gentiles!) rejected the call to join the new community of faith.

A fourth reason not to consider Luke-Acts anti-Semitic is the *universal* aspect of the call to conversion. If Luke blames the Jews for acting out of ignorance, he also indicates that the Gentiles live in ignorance as well, as Paul indicates in his speech at the Areopagus in front of the altar "To an Unknown God" (17:23). Paul explicitly states that "God has overlooked the *times of ignorance,* but now he demands that *all people everywhere repent.* . ." (17:30). The disciples' call to conversion is thus universal and bi-directional. Through the resurrection God designated Jesus "as leader and savior to grant Israel *repentance and forgiveness of sins*" (5:31), and Paul's ministry demonstrates the universal movement "first to those in Damascus and in Jerusalem and throughout the whole country of Judea, and then to the Gentiles," and that the messiah would "proclaim light both to our people and to the Gentiles" (26:20, 23). If Acts indicates that the Gentiles become more responsive than the Jews to the apostles' message, it is not for purposes of promoting anti-Semitic or anti-Jewish sentiment. It is to indicate how the direction of the church changed in the course of history and how universal it became. These four reasons provide some reason for caution when interpreting apparent anti-Jewish passages in Luke-Acts.

Individual Stories of Conversion

An appealing part of Acts is the number of memorable conversion stories about individuals who become key stones in the larger mosaic of Christianity's growth. In some ways, the whole book might be considered as a series of conversions, both individual and communal, which describe the spread of the gospel to the ends of the earth. Acts contains idealized summary passages that make general statements such as, "And every day the Lord added to their number those who were being saved" (2:47b; cf. 16:5), to give the impression of constant conversions, but the individual conversion stories contain the most significant information.

Scholars generally point to five prominent accounts of individual conversion stories in Acts. These are the Ethiopian eunuch (8:26–40); Paul (9:1–19; 22:6–16; 26:12–18); Cornelius (10:1—11:18; 15:7–11); Lydia (16:14–15); and the Philippian jailer (16:25–34). Curiously, the traditional Greek vocabulary of conversion is absent from each of these stories (Löffler 1975: 35), but we have seen before that such language need not always be present to portray conversion. Stephen Smalley (1964: 200–201) has compared these accounts and noted that they contain a relatively consistent pattern incorporating six stages of conversion. (1) There is always some form of *preparation* for the conversion. (2) Mediators *preach* about Jesus in some fashion. (3) The individuals make *inquiry*. (4) There is usually evidence of *God's activity* in the conversion. (5) *Baptism* is uniformly mentioned. (6) Each conversion entails specific though not uniform *results*.

Of the six stages, the most important is baptism because of its consistent mention in these conversion contexts and because of its inherent connection to faith. Baptism leads to faith in Jesus Christ. But baptism is not explicitly mentioned in every case. In two specific locations Luke connects conversion broadly with coming to faith in Jesus. The first is in the description of the church at Antioch where the disciples "were first called Christians" (11:26): "The hand of the Lord was with them and a great number who *believed turned* to the Lord (11:21). A second reference is in Paul's farewell speech at Miletus, where he testifies, "I earnestly bore witness for both Jews and Greeks to *repentance* before God and to *faith* in our Lord Jesus" (20:21). Repentance leads to faith, and baptism is the normal means of coming to faith in Acts. By baptism is meant not only John the Baptist's "baptism for repentance" (13:24; 19:4), but the baptism of water *and* the Holy Spirit, the empowerment to become a disciple of Jesus Christ.

Because of their importance in shaping the total vision of conversion in Acts, we will examine briefly each of the five stories of individual conversions.

The Ethiopian Eunuch (8:26–40)

The first story of individual conversion in Acts concerns a foreigner, clearly a Gentile, who is probably a "Godfearer" (cf. 10:2), i.e., a non-Jew who accepted most aspects of Judaism and attended synagogue worship but did not adhere to circumcision or certain dietary regulations. The text first makes it clear that God is guiding the story by mentioning three elements. An "angel of the Lord" (v. 26) instructs Philip to head into the desert toward Gaza, the Holy Spirit instructs him to catch up to the eunuch's chariot, and after the conversion Philip miraculously disappears. As with all conversions, this is an act of God:

> [30]Philip ran up and heard him reading Isaiah the prophet and said, "Do you *understand* what you are reading?" [31]He replied, "How can I, unless someone instructs me?" So he invited Philip to get in and sit with him. [32]This was the scripture passage he was reading:
>
> "Like a sheep he was led to the slaughter,
> and as a lamb before its shearer is silent,
>   so he opened not his mouth.
> [33]In [his] humiliation justice was denied him.
>   Who will tell of his posterity?
>   For his life is taken from the earth."
>
> [34]Then the eunuch said to Philip in reply, "I beg you, about whom is the prophet saying this? About himself, or about someone else?" [35]Then Philip *opened his mouth* and, beginning with this scripture passage, he *proclaimed Jesus* to him. [36]As they traveled along the road they came to some *water,* and the eunuch said, "Look, there is water. What is to prevent my being *baptized?"* [38]Then he ordered the chariot to stop, and Philip and the eunuch both went down into the water, and he *baptized* him. [39]When they came out of the water, the Spirit of the Lord snatched Philip away, and the eunuch saw him no more, but continued on his way *rejoicing* (8:30–39).

This simple but profound story contains various elements characteristic of Luke. The conversion is initiated by God but mediated by an apostle.[52] It overcomes ignorance and leads to baptism by water and action of the Holy Spirit. It furthermore involves the explanation of scripture (cf. Luke 24:27) which overcomes the individual's ignorance, is christocentric (that is, leading to faith in Jesus), and concludes on a note of joy. But of primary importance is that the figure who is converted is a Gentile, albeit one who is prepared for conversion because he is already sensitized to faith issues by virtue of being a Godfearer. As with other conversion stories, this one is at the service of Luke's larger picture of salvation history—God's plan is to make salvation universal and not narrowly focused upon Israel as the chosen people.

Paul (9:1–19; 22:6–16; 26:12–18)

By far the most impressive and memorable conversion story in Acts is that of Paul, the apostle to the Gentiles. The sheer repetition of the story three times is enough to indicate its importance from Luke's perspective. Most scholars have viewed the repetitions as both for emphasis and the result of different sources. But it may also be part of a narrative strategy (which I have elsewhere termed "functional redundancy") to emphasize how significant the turning to the Gentiles really is.[53] Limitations of space will prevent us from examining each of these three passages in depth, but we will use the narrative of Acts 9 as a control to comment on the importance of Paul's conversion because it is the first of the three accounts and is described by means of third person narration.

Whenever anyone thinks of Paul's "Damascus road" incident, probably one of any dozen artistic portrayals comes to mind of a stubborn and zealous Paul lying on the road beside his horse, gazing into a blinding light from heaven. One also thinks of Flannery O'Connor's famous line, "I reckon the Lord knew that the only way to make a Christian out of that one was to knock him off his horse."[54] Alas, the horse is a figment of renaissance artistic imagination (Acts never mentions *how* Paul was traveling to Damascus), and scholars are not at all agreed that what Paul underwent was a "conversion." This is indicative of the confusion which exists about the NT understanding of conversion. If by conversion is meant changing religions, symbolized by a name change (as well as interior and exterior attitudes), then Paul is not a convert! Even after the Damascus road incident Paul is still portrayed as a faithful Jew who happens to believe in Jesus as the messiah. And nowhere does Acts indicate that his name was changed in the process. Acts 13:9 merely states that Saul was "also known as Paul," conforming to the common first-century practice of Jews having both a Jewish and Hellenistic-Roman name. For these and other reasons some scholars prefer to speak of Paul's "call" rather than conversion.[55] But we have already seen that the NT does not conceive of conversion only in terms of changing religions. Indeed, it is a much broader reality which is more often directed to believing disciples than to non-believers. Suffice it to say that, in the case of Paul, while there are definitely elements of a prophetic "call" (cf. 2:39) in his personal story, it is also possible to speak of true conversion, for the two cannot be completely separated (Hulsbosch 1966: 74).

One of the primary images Acts uses to describe Paul's conversion is the movement from blindness to sight.[56] Paul's story is of a violently zealous persecutor of Christians who suddenly finds his eyes opened to a new work, the work of the Lord:

> [3]On his journey, as he was nearing Damascus, a *light* from the sky suddenly flashed around him. [4]He fell to the ground and heard a voice saying to him, "Saul, Saul, why are you persecuting me?" [5]He said, "Who are you, sir?" The reply came, "I am Jesus, whom you are persecuting. [6]Now get up and go into the city and you will be told what you must do." [7]The men traveling with him stood speechless, for they heard the voice but could see no one. [8]Saul got up from the ground, but when he *opened his eyes* he *could see nothing;* so they led him by the hand and brought him to Damascus. [9]For three days he was *unable to see,* and he neither ate nor drank.
>
> [10]There was a disciple in Damascus named Ananaias, and the Lord said to him in a vision, "Ananaias." He answered, "Here I am, Lord." [11]The Lord said to him, "Get up and go to the street called Straight and ask at the house of Judas for a man from Tarsus named Saul. He is there praying, [12]and [in a vision] he has seen a man named Ananaias come in and lay [his] hands on him, that he may *regain his sight."* [13]But Ananaias replied, "Lord, I have heard from many sources about this man, what *evil things* he has done to your holy ones in Jerusalem.

¹⁴And here he has authority from the chief priests to imprison all who call upon your name." ¹⁵But the Lord said to him, "Go, for this man is a *chosen instrument* of mine *to carry my name before Gentiles, kings, and Israelites,* ¹⁶and I will show him what he will have to suffer for my name." ¹⁷So Ananaias went and entered the house; laying his hands on him, he said, "Saul, my brother, the Lord has sent me, Jesus who appeared to you on the way by which you came, that you may *regain your sight* and be filled with the holy Spirit." ¹⁸Immediately, *things like scales fell from his eyes* and *he regained his sight.* He got up and was baptized, ¹⁹and when he had eaten, he recovered his strength (9:3–19).

The movement from blindness to sight permeates Paul's conversion. The blindness is not only Paul's self-induced stubbornness in not realizing how wrong he is to persecute "the Way," but it is also a divinely caused blindness, as seen in the external causes. The light is "from the sky" and when he is healed, "things like scales" fall off his eyes. His blindness is thus for a divine purpose, to reveal Paul as a "chosen instrument" to evangelize the Gentiles. The reversal of the expected order of evangelization from Israel to the Gentiles, placing the Gentiles first (9:15; cf. 1:8), emphasizes Paul's mission. He who was zealous *against* the Lord now becomes zealous *for* the Lord.

Various redundant features as the story is repeated in Acts 22 and 26 contribute to understanding Paul's conversion in this fashion. Each time the story is told, the brightness of the light is magnified (cf. 9:3; 22:6; 26:13) to emphasize the divine source of conversion. Each repetition of the story diminishes Ananaias' role of mediation (cf. 9:10–17; 22:12–16) until he is entirely absent in 26:12–18. The effect of this is to heighten the immediacy of Paul's conversion and commission by the Lord. Finally, each version of the story expands the instruction to Paul about his mission as apostle to the Gentiles (cf. 9:15–16; 22:14–15; 26:16–18).

The challenge issued to Paul to go to the Gentiles reaches its apex in Acts 26, where Paul says he received his commission not from Ananaias but from the Risen Lord himself:

"I have appeared to you for this purpose, to appoint you as a *servant* and *witness* to what you have seen [of me] and what you will be shown. [17]I shall deliver you from this people and from the *Gentiles* to whom I send you, [18]to *open their eyes* that they may *turn from darkness to light* and *from the power of Satan to God,* so that they may obtain *forgiveness of sins* and an inheritance among those who have been consecrated by *faith in me"* (26:16–18; cf. 26:20, 23).

This passage defines most clearly the purpose of Paul's conversion. He, whose own eyes have been opened by God, must now go to the Gentiles to open their eyes. He is to be a servant and witness (*martys;* also 22:15),[57] and his ministry is described by three interrelated images, turning the Gentiles from "darkness to light," from Satan's power to God's power, and facilitating "forgiveness of sins." One could not hope for a better description of the result of conversion from Luke's perspective. It brings people to faith, forgives their sins, brings them to God's power as people who are led from darkness to light. This transformation is an experience of salvation as is apparent in Paul and Barnabas' earlier words in Acts: "For so the Lord has commanded us, 'I have made you a *light* to the Gentiles, so that you may be an instrument of *salvation* to the ends of the earth'" (13:47). Paul's conversion, then, makes him one of the premier examples of conversion in Acts, but he is one of a long list of those who experience a drastic transformation in their lives.

Cornelius (Acts 10:1—11:18; 15:7-11)

The third major conversion story in Acts, also narrated several times and with a brief reprise in Acts 15, is that of the Roman centurion, Cornelius. His story (10:1–8, 22, 30–33; 11:11–14) is intertwined with a repeated vision to Peter (10:9–16; 11:5–10) about clean and unclean foods. It is also part of this pattern in Acts of defending the mission to the Gentiles using the literary technique of functional redundancy.[58] The length of the narrative prohibits reproducing the entire story; instead, I will provide summary comments.

The very context, following closely on the heels of Paul's conversion in Acts 9, sets the stage for interpreting Cornelius' conversion. Peter becomes the major figure in this story who facilitates the movement to the Gentiles, for Cornelius' role is actually symbolic. Two brief scenes occur prior to Acts 10 which show the success Peter has in converting others. At Lydda and Sharon (9:32–35) Peter accomplishes a healing which leads to conversion: ". . .and they *turned* to the Lord" (9:35). At Joppa, Peter accomplishes another miracle which leads to conversion: ". . . and many came *to believe* in the Lord" (9:42). The context for conversion is set as Cornelius becomes not simply an individual convert but a symbol of the Gentile world coming to faith in Jesus Christ.

As is common in Acts, Cornelius is described as "ripe" for conversion by virtue of his character. He is devout, a Godfearer, an almsgiver, and one who constantly prayed (10:2). He receives a divine vision telling him to seek out Peter who, by staying in the house of a tanner (9:43), considered an unclean profession, already hints at the coming conversion. Ironically, Cornelius is not the only one who is the object of conversion. Peter's vision about the unclean animals, repeated twice but said to have occurred three times (10:16), indicates that he, too, needs to learn, "What God has made clean, you are not to call profane" (10:15). This story is as much about Peter's conversion to the view that "God shows no partiality" (10:34) as it is the conversion of a Godfearer and his household to Jesus.

The actual conversion story is recounted after Peter goes to Cornelius' household and preaches a mini-gospel (10:34–43):

> ⁴⁴"While Peter was still speaking these things, the holy Spirit fell upon *all* who were listening to the word. ⁴⁵The circumcised believers who had accompanied Peter were astounded that the *gift* of the holy Spirit should have been poured out on the Gentiles also, ⁴⁶for they could hear them speaking in tongues and glorifying God. Then Peter responded, ⁴⁷"Can anyone withhold the water for *baptizing these people,* who have received the holy Spirit even as we have?" ⁴⁸He ordered them to be baptized in the name of Jesus Christ. ⁴⁹Then they invited him to stay for a few days (10:44–48).

Note that the coming of the Spirit is described as a "gift" and that it precedes baptism (cf. 9:17–18) but is intimately linked to it. For Luke, while the Holy Spirit is essential to conversion, it is not always a result of baptism but can be a prelude to it. It is also important to see how the conversion of "all" who are in Cornelius' household (cf. 10:2; 11:14) emphasizes that the conversion is symbolic of the Gentiles over and above the person of Cornelius (who is never even named in 11:11-14!).

Moreover, this double conversion (Cornelius' and Peter's) results in mutual hospitality (cf. 10:23, 49), a significant theme in Luke-Acts and the heart of the controversy when Peter is challenged on the grounds of his social interaction with Gentiles.[59] The Jewish believers in Jerusalem specifically challenge him: "You entered the house of uncircumcised people and ate with them" (11:3). For Luke, true conversion leads to mutual hospitality symbolic of human reconciliation. God's gift of salvation cannot be limited to a few chosen ones, but is a wide gift given to all who embrace the gospel message. Ultimately, the objectors are mollified by Peter's defense of his actions, and they conclude, "God has then granted life-giving *repentance* to the Gentiles too" (11:18). This perspective on Cornelius' conversion is confirmed by both Peter and James at the council of Jerusalem, where the direction to continue to evangelize the Gentiles is affirmed (15:7-9, 13-19). Cornelius' conversion, then, becomes symbolic of the entire direction Acts takes to spread the good news to the ends of the earth.

Lydia (16:14-15); The Philippian Jailer (16:25-34); and Other Tales

Two briefer accounts of individual conversions are found in Acts, and they essentially reinforce what we have seen thus far. One case is Lydia, a wealthy woman,[60] whose entire household is baptized and who offers hospitality to Paul and his companions. Another is the unnamed jailer at Philippi who, upon the conversion of himself and his entire household, also offers hospitality to Paul and Silas. In both cases the pattern we have discussed above is apparent.

Normally, these five are considered the only major stories of conversion in Acts. In addition, however, there are other conversion stories mentioned which may function as negative examples. One such case is the proconsul, Sergius Paulus, who "wanted to hear the word of God" from Barnabas and Saul (13:7):

> [8]But Elymas the magician (for that is what his name means) opposed them in an attempt to *turn* the proconsul *away from the faith.* [9]But Saul, also known as Paul, filled with the holy Spirit, looked intently at him [10]and said, "You son of the devil, you enemy of all that is right, full of every sort of deceit and fraud. Will you not stop twisting the *straight* paths of [the] Lord? [11]Even now the hand of the Lord is upon you. You will be *blind,* and *unable to see* the sun for a time." Immediately a *dark mist* [literally, "mist and darkness"] fell upon him, and he went about seeking people to lead him by the hand. [12]When the proconsul saw what had happened, he *came to believe,* for he was astonished at the teaching about the Lord (13:8–12).

It is obviously important for Luke that such a highly placed Roman figure as a proconsul would be converted, but there is more to this story than apologetics. In effect, this story shows Paul ironically acting out his own conversion in reverse fashion! A man (enamored of "magic") who seeks to pervert the gospel by "turning" someone away from faith finds himself blinded, "unable to see," living in "darkness," and looking for someone to "lead him by the hand" (cf. the description of Saul in 9:8–9) because he is "twisting the straight paths of [the] Lord." Paul, who lived on "Straight Street" (9:11) after his Damascus road incident here shows how important it is to see conversion as changing a twisted life. Elymas serves as much as a negative example of conversion as Sergius Paulus serves as a positive example. Opposing the gift of faith can lead to dire consequences. Elymas himself is described in a way that makes *him* a candidate for conversion.

A second example is given in the story of yet another magician, Simon Magus (8:9–24). Many scholars would not consider this story to be an important illustration of conversion because Simon is ultimately cursed by Peter when he tries to *buy* the gift of the Spirit (vv. 18–20). However, the story occurs in the context of the successful conversion of Samaritans (vv. 14, 25), and Simon himself is said to have "believed" and been "baptized" (v. 13). In the end, although Simon is explicitly exhorted, "Repent of this wickedness" (v. 22), the story never says whether or not Peter's curse takes effect. Rather, it ends on an ambiguous note with Simon's plea to Peter: "Pray for me to the Lord, that nothing of what you have said may come upon me" (v. 24). The purpose of the story vis-à-vis conversion is twofold. In the first place, conversion is not a "magical" event involving manipulation of supernatural powers by some magical formula. In the second place, conversion is not something one can buy, literally or figuratively. It is a gift of God, given with baptism and the Holy Spirit and demanding a drastic change in life. From this perspective, Simon Magus is at the very least a good counterfigure of conversion.

Summary

The above evidence shows that the Acts of the Apostles contains an extensive and complex understanding of conversion. While it is consistent with the Gospel of Luke, it nonetheless expands its understanding considerably. Hazardous as it may be to try to synthesize this material into some valid generalizations, we can describe the major features of how the book of Acts views conversion.

1) Conversion involves recognizing one's sinfulness and the need for a dramatic change of direction in life. Without a sense of neediness and an act of repentance, conversion cannot occur, because God does not *force* conversion on anybody.

2) Conversion is a precious gift from God, accompanied by baptism and the Holy Spirit. God is always the initiator of conversion. It brings salvation and forgiveness of sins. It usually takes place in response to having heard God's Word, i.e., the Scriptures themselves and the preaching or testimony of others who serve as mediators of the process. Christian conversion always leads to *faith* in Jesus Christ and the attendant task to become a servant and witness of this faith.

3) Rather than being an end in and of itself, conversion in Acts is just a *beginning*. Conversion results in concrete outward changes of behavior. It overcomes ignorance and stubbornness, and it leads to rejoicing and glorifying God, to warm hospitality, and

to universal evangelization among all people to become a part of the new Christian community.

4) Although conversion takes place in groups, it is also an individualized reality. Individuals *within* groups must hear the Word of God and be converted to the gospel.

5) Conversion is described as the movement from blindness to sight. Indeed, many descriptions of conversions in history frequently use this language.[61] It is as if a spiritual blindfold is suddenly lifted and one can see with new vision what was not perceived prior to the conversion. Related images are also prominent. People in need of conversion are living in dark shadows, walking down crooked paths. They need to move from darkness to light, from the crooked ways of Satan to the straight ways of God.

6) Conversion does involve universal outreach to non-believers and often involves movement from paganism to Christianity, but it does not always involve a change of "religion" per se. Instead, Acts emphasizes that many who undergo conversion are already prepared for it, leading God-fearing and ethically correct lives, but still needing to come to full faith in Jesus Christ. Conversion sometimes but not always comes like a bolt out of the blue. From this perspective, even members of a faith community can remain in need of deeper conversion, and wrongheaded believers (e.g., Paul as persecutor) need a shocking turnabout to set them on the right path.

We have thus seen how Acts relates to Luke's Gospel in discussing conversion and how the concept is nuanced and expanded. If one were to seek a convenient shorthand description of conversion in Luke-Acts, you could do no better than to sing a stanza of the traditional song, "Amazing Grace":

> Amazing grace! how sweet the sound,
> That saved a wretch like me!
> I once was lost, but now am found,
> Was blind, but now I see.

As comfortable as we may be with the view of conversion in Acts, we should be reminded that it is but one NT description. We move now to the Gospel of John and its own unique perspective.

6

Conversion in John:
From Darkness to Light

The notion of conversion in the Acts of the Apostles was captured by the image of "blindness-to-sight." In the Gospel of John, the primary image is "darkness-to-light." These are certainly interrelated images in both Acts (see Gaventa 1986) and John. In fact, the titles of the previous chapter and the present one could in some ways be switched without great damage to either book of the NT. Yet John does not simply dish up warmed over Lukan concepts on the conversion plate. With the Fourth Gospel, a whole new menu is offered.[62]

The Gospel of John has always been recognized as quite different from the Synoptic Gospels. Clement of Alexandria called it "the spiritual Gospel," and it is often seen as more ethereal, less practical, and often more mysterious than its companion Gospels. Despite this, it may come as quite a surprise that the language of conversion which we discussed in chapter one is totally absent from John. Nowhere does John use the typical vocabulary of conversion (*metanoeō, epistrephō* and cognates) except at 12:40, the quote from Isaiah 6 we examined above (pp. 19–20). Neither the message of John the Baptist nor Jesus expresses teaching about conversion in ways we have come to expect in the NT. Does this mean that John has no concept of conversion or is simply not interested in the topic? By no means! But to get at the concept we must enter the mysterious Johannine world and explore this new territory by way of a different but related vocabulary. The first clues are given in the prologue to the Gospel (1:1–18).

Unlike Mark, who starts his Gospel with John the Baptist's ministry, and unlike Matthew and Luke, who each have infancy narratives, John begins his Gospel with a poetic prologue on a cosmic scale. With grandiose talk about the "beginning" (a direct allusion to Genesis 1:1), John waxes eloquently about the eternal "Word" who is life and light (1:4). An overarching motif, which becomes so prominent in understanding the Johannine concept of conversion, is the contrast between light and darkness. ". . .[T]he light shines in the darkness, and the darkness has not overcome it" (1:5). Interspersed with this poetic vision is the narrative of John the Baptist: "He was not the light but came to testify to the light" (1:8).[63] As John sees it, the challenge for people is to accept the light, become children of the light, and to avoid darkness. It is an ethical dualism reminiscent of Jewish intertestamental literature and the writings of Qumran, but which is explicitly applied to the significance of Jesus, the "Word-made-flesh" (1:14). He descends to the world as its savior, bringing light, truth, life, and love, and ascends again to his heavenly Father (cf. 4:42; 20:17).

From Darkness to Light

To see how pervasive this theme of light and darkness in John is, we will look at a few key passages. Of major importance is Jesus' own self-revelation: "I am the *light* of the world. Whoever follows me will not walk in *darkness,* but will have the *light* of life" (8:12; cf. 1 John 1:5–7). Despite this self-revelation, and characteristic of John's Gospel, the characters in the story fail to recognize his identity. So he must cite his teaching often and with almost tedious repetition:

> [35]"The *light* will be among you only a little while. Walk while you have the *light,* so that *darkness* may not overcome you. Whoever walks in the *dark* does not know where he is going. [36]While you have the *light, believe* in the *light,* so that you may become children of the *light.* . . ."[46]I came into the world as

> *light,* so that everyone who *believes* in me might not remain
> in *darkness''* (12:35-36, 46; cf. 1:9; 11:9-10).

That this imagery is more than just metaphorical rhetoric becomes clear when it is strongly attached to faith (belief) and when
its ethical relation to good and evil is enunciated:

> [16]For God so loved the world that he *gave* his only Son, so that
> everyone who *believes* in him might not perish but might have
> eternal life. . . .[18]Whoever *believes* in him will not be con-
> demned, but whoever does not *believe* has already been con-
> demned, because he has not *believed* in the name of the only
> Son of God. [19]And this is the verdict, that the *light* came into
> the world, but people preferred *darkness* to *light,* because their
> works are *evil.* [20]For everyone who does *wicked things* hates
> the *light* and does not come toward the *light,* so that his works
> might not be exposed. [21]But whoever lives the truth comes to
> the *light,* so that his works may be clearly seen as done in God
> (3:16, 18-21).

The contrast in this passage shows that light and darkness are tied
to concrete human actions. Darkness represents doing evil deeds
(1 John 2:9), and light represents righteous deeds which reflect
conformity to God's desire for the universe. The light is pure gift
from God which brings people to faith, provided they respond
with proper testimony and "works."

Another prominent aspect of this passage is a theme reflecting
the heart of conversion for John. It concerns belief in Jesus or
coming to faith (cf. also 1 John 3:23; 5:5). Belief is not a static
idea but a very active, dynamic force, shown by the preference
to use the verb "to believe" rather than the noun, "faith." This
theme is already apparent in the midst of the prologue in a short
passage I take to be central to John's perspective on conversion:

> [12]But to those who did accept him he gave power to become
> children of God, to those who *believe* in his name, [13]who were
> *born* not by natural generation nor by human choice nor by
> a man's decision but *of God* (1:12-13).

John's Gospel emphasizes the need to *believe* in Jesus, the incar-
nate Word. This passage is so central to John's understanding

because it summarizes the need to be "born" entirely through God's power. Only those "begotten of God" are victorious in life, and "the victory that conquers the world is our faith" (1 John 5:4-5).

The purpose of the Gospel, in fact, as stated near the conclusion, is proclaimed forthrightly in terms of faith, placing one's total belief in Jesus Christ. The Gospel has been "written that you may [come to] *believe* that Jesus is the Messiah, the Son of God, and that *through this belief* you may have *life* in his name" (20:31). The expression in brackets ("come to") indicates the possibility of reading this passage as evidence that John was written as a missionary tract to convert people to the Christian faith. However, along with most scholars, I prefer to read the Gospel as a tract written for Christian believers who are faced with certain problems about remaining faithful to their beliefs. Either way, John is clear that faith in Jesus is the *goal* of his Gospel and this faith means "concrete obedience" to the Father's will which produces new life (Löffler 1975: 37).

John the Baptist and Conversion

In the other Gospels we saw how John the Baptist was connected with conversion because he was associated with a baptism of repentance. Since such terminology is missing from the Fourth Gospel, one can ask whether John the Baptist has in any fashion a role to play in John's perspective of conversion. Actually, this provides us another opportunity to see just how different this Gospel's understanding really is.

John the Baptist is a prominent figure at the beginning of the Fourth Gospel but his role vis-à-vis Jesus is distinctive. Although he baptizes with water (1:26, 33), it is an act not explicitly associated with forgiveness of sin. Instead, John's proper role is to *testify*[64] to Jesus whom he explicitly identifies as "the Lamb of God who takes away the sin of the world" (1:29, 36). John's main task is to point (literally and figuratively) to Jesus as the one in whom God's will for the salvation of the world is centered. John's limited ministry is thus preliminary to Jesus, but he is no Elijah figure (1:21, 25). He comes on stage for a short time and exits quickly so as not to detract from the main character. As he says of Jesus and himself, "He must increase; I must decrease" (3:30).[65]

John's designation of Jesus as the lamb of God is more than an OT allusion to the Passover lamb (Exod 12) or to the "suffering servant" figure (Isa 53:7, 10). It is also a prefigurement of Jesus' own sacrifice on the cross, for unlike the Synoptic Gospels, John records that Jesus was crucified on the "preparation day" at noon just when the Passover lambs were slaughtered for the great feast (19:14). Jesus, the good shepherd who lays down his own life freely (10:11), ironically dies as an innocent lamb to become salvation for the whole world.

In the Fourth Gospel, the whole focus on forgiveness of sin is christologically oriented. The *person of Jesus,* rather than the message, becomes the focus for forgiveness of sin. Even the use of the singular (sin) rather than the plural (sins) hints at the importance of sin as a power in the world that needs to be conquered (Cothenet 1989: 58). Thus the cosmic dimension of the battle between light and darkness is carried over into the confrontation between sin and goodness. Jesus is the one who overcomes Satan and sin in the world because he is the truth (14:6) and the light that cannot be overcome by darkness (1:5; cf. 14:30; 16:33).

John the Baptist's role, then, is to focus attention on Jesus as the key figure in conversion. Although John's Gospel does not have a systematic way of speaking of conversion, there are three major passages where aspects of conversion take center stage as individuals encounter the person of Jesus.[66] These are Nicodemus (3:1–20), the Samaritan woman (4:7–42), and the man born blind (9:1–41). We will examine each of these in turn.

Nicodemus (3:1–20)

Nicodemus is described as a Pharisee and "ruler of the Jews" (3:1) who is said to come to Jesus "at night" (3:2; cf. 19:39). The mention of night, with its connotations of darkness and sinister activity, is indicative of Nicodemus' neediness as regards conversion. For John, night is symbolic of doing evil deeds (such as Judas, 13:30) and needing light (9:4). By coming at night Nicodemus no doubt avoids ridicule from his peers for seeking out Jesus, but he also shows that he is one who truly needs to be "enlightened." Nicodemus respectfully addresses Jesus and comments on the marvelous "signs"[67] which he is doing:

> [3]Jesus answered and said to him, "Amen, amen, I say to you, no one can see the kingdom of God without being *born from above.*" [4]Nicodemus said to him, "How can a person once grown old be *born again?* Surely he cannot reenter his mother's womb and be *born again,* can he?" [5]Jesus answered, "Amen, amen, I say to you, no one can enter the kingdom of God without being *born of water and Spirit.* [6]What is born of *flesh* is flesh and what is born of *spirit* is spirit. [7]Do not be amazed that I told you, 'You[68] must be *born from above.*' [8]The *wind* blows where it wills, and you can hear the sound it makes, but you do not know where it comes from or where it goes; so it is with everyone who is born of the Spirit" (3:3–8).

This passage is filled with Johannine images and concerns. What begins as a dialogue becomes a monologue (cf. also 3:10–15). This passage, in fact, is the first of many discourses which Jesus makes in the Gospel. Nicodemus misinterprets Jesus' words ("born from above"), which in Greek can also mean born "again" (*anōthen*), and thinks that Jesus is talking about a medical miracle of reentering his mother's womb. Instead, Jesus is trying to get at the distinction between this world and its limitations (represented by "flesh") and the divine world from whence Jesus comes (represented by "spirit"). A further play on the word "spirit," which in Greek and Hebrew can also mean "wind," indicates just how mysterious this rebirth process really is. Because it is God's power, one cannot see it tangibly but one can experience it fully. One can neither "see" nor "enter" God's kingdom without being born *from above.*

This may well be the most famous passage in the NT concerning conversion because it has become the centerpiece of evangelical Protestant teaching. These are the "born again" Christians who emphasize this passage as *the* crucial one indicating the absolute requirement of Christians to have a specific moment of conversion in which they experience a rebirth. The allusion to baptism by the mention of "water and the Spirit" supports this interpretation. But how central to the NT teaching on conversion is this passage? This question calls for several comments.

The first thing to note is the infrequency of "born again" language both in John and the rest of the NT. This is the *only* passage where the phrase appears (but cf. similar language in 1 John 3:9; 4:7; 5:1, 4, 18; Gal 4:23, 29; 1 Pet 1:3). It seems precipitous at best to make this expression *the* hallmark of conversion when there are so many other NT expressions which are more numerous and prominent.

A second comment concerns the *context* in which this phrase is used. Although grammatically the Greek can mean "from above" or "again," the context clearly favors the former, while the latter represents Nicodemus' misunderstanding which Jesus proceeds to correct. It is the contrast between flesh and spirit, between "earthly things" and "heavenly things" (3:12), which Nicodemus is being challenged to recognize. In his encounter with Jesus Nicodemus is beginning a movement out of darkness into light so that he may "believe" and be a recipient of "eternal life" (3:15). When the adjective *anōthen* is used elsewhere in John (3:31, 19:11) it also has the same connotation of this contrast between the spiritual, heavenly world and our world here "below."[69] In short, the expression "born from above" (cf. 1 John 5:4, "begotten by God") is John's way of challenging the priorities people have in life. They must put the things of God first if they wish to receive the fullness of life (10:10; cf. 5:40).

A third factor is the secondary sacramental symbolism in this passage.[70] It is quite typical of John to indicate interest in sacramental symbolism (e.g., John 6 and the Eucharist), but these interests are generally secondary in the text. In this case the symbolism of baptism is surely present (Cothenet 1989: 61), but the primary concern of the text is christological in nature (as indicated also by the reference to Jesus being "lifted up" on the cross, v. 14; cf. 8:28; 12:32, 34). Nicodemus is never shown being baptized nor does he figure prominently in the Johannine community. But he is a figure who encounters Jesus and comes to at least partial faith in him. Rather than having one moment of conversion, his faith seems to grow slowly throughout the Gospel, as indicated by two other references. Nicodemus is shown timidly defending Jesus before the Jewish leaders (7:50–51), and in the passion account he is bold enough to assist in the burial of Jesus' body (19:39). While he is not a shining model disciple, he nonetheless shows growth in discipleship. In the end, as beautiful as the "born again" image is, it is but one part of the complex NT teaching on conversion.

Finally, if the Gospel (as indicated above) was written for believers rather than for non-believers, the significance of being "born again" is the ongoing nature of this call. It reminds me of a comic strip I once saw in which one character says to another, "I'm born again." The other responds, "Well, I'm born again, and again, and again, and again. . . ." The challenge is continually to renew one's faith in Jesus so that it never has a chance to grow stale.

What does this passage say about conversion? It is the result of an encounter with Jesus and being "born from above." It is a reception of water and the Spirit and a transformation of life from darkness to light, from the finite to the infinite. It leads to faith and to *eternal* life.[71]

The Samaritan Woman (4:7–42)

The next important passage on conversion functions almost as a second panel of a medieval diptych. Whereas Nicodemus was a *man* in a position of authority, part of the established Jewish powers, this next figure is an *unnamed woman* belonging to the despised class of Samaritans and part of the great mass of underprivileged of Jesus' day. They are a study in contrasts, and yet each is changed by the encounter with Jesus.

This story is another fine example of Johannine subtlety built on a misunderstanding which Jesus helps clarify, utilizing a pun. The simplicity of the story belies its depth. It is actually a story of gradual conversion in four stages:

> [7]A woman of Samaria came to draw water. Jesus said to her, *"Give me a drink."* [8]His disciples had gone into the town to buy food. [9]The Samaritan woman said to him, "How can you, a Jew, ask me, a Samaritan woman, for a drink?" (For Jews use nothing in common with Samaritans.) [10]Jesus answered and said to her, "If you knew the *gift of God* and who is saying to you, 'Give me a drink,' you would have asked him and he

would have given you *living water.*" [11][The woman] said to him,
"Sir, you do not even have a bucket and the cistern is deep;
where then can you get this *living water?* [12]Are you greater than
our father Jacob, who gave us this cistern and drank from it
himself with his children and his flocks?" [13]Jesus answered and
said to her, "Everyone who drinks this water will be thirsty;
[14]but whoever drinks the water I shall give will never thirst; the
water I shall give will become in him a *spring of water* welling
up to *eternal life.*" [15]The woman said to him, "Sir, *give me
this water,* so that I may not be thirsty or have to keep coming
here to draw water" (4:7-15).

The overwhelming water imagery in this first stage revolves
around a pun on the meaning of "living water," which can refer
either to running water or more profoundly, supernatural water.
The narrative begins, as is quite typical in John, with Jesus' initiative (cf. 1:38; 6:5). Ironically, he seems to be seeking her help
when, in fact, she is the one who needs *his* help. She does not
yet recognize that in front of her is God's "gift" to the world
(cf. 3:16). She is incredulous that Jesus is even speaking to her,
a woman and a Samaritan (cf. the disciples' incredulity as well,
4:27). She also has difficulty understanding that the water Jesus
refers to is not physical water but spiritual water from an eternal
source. This section concludes with a turnabout. She who was
asked for water now asks Jesus for water. Stage one of her conversion is established.

The second stage results from their continued dialogue over the
fact that she has "no husband" (4:17). But when Jesus points
out that she has had five husbands, her response takes her another stage on the process of conversion: "Sir, I can see that you
are a *prophet*" (4:19).

A third stage develops as Jesus instructs her about the nature
of true worship of the Father, which is "in Spirit and truth"
(4:23). When Jesus reveals to her that he is the awaited messiah
(4:26), she promptly leaves her water jar (symbolic of her lack
of needing well water now)[72] and goes to her town to invite others
to come and see the one who is "possibly" the *messiah* (4:28-
30). Her faith is slowly deepening as she realizes more and more
Jesus' true identity.

Then the final stage reached as the result of this personal encounter is narrated:

> ³⁹Many of the Samaritans of that town began to *believe* in him *because of the word of the woman who testified,* "He told me everything I have done." ⁴⁰When the Samaritans came to him, they invited him to stay with them; and he stayed there two days. ⁴¹Many more began to *believe in him because of his word,* ⁴²and they said to the woman, "We no longer *believe because of your word;* for we have heard for ourselves, and we know that this truly is the *savior of the world"* (4:39-42).

The woman's faith reaches its apex when her *testimony* mediates others' coming to faith. Not just any "others" but Samaritans, representative of the wider non-Jewish world. The diptych comes full circle as this story shows that Jesus is not only savior for the Jews (the Nicodemus story; cf. 4:22) but also non-Jews, ultimately the savior of the *world.*[73] As important as her own conversion is in leading others to faith, even more important from John's perspective is that her colleagues eventually come to faith themselves by their own personal encounter with Jesus Christ (cf. 20:29).

What does this passage tell us about conversion? For John, it is a response to the revelation of Jesus, a gradual process of recognition of his identity and mission as savior of the world. It comes from a personal encounter with Jesus but can begin with the testimony of others who believe. It is meant for *all* who thirst for something more in life. Again, baptismal imagery is in the background and is an essential element of the passage, but its secondary nature does not overshadow the more prominent christological import of the Samaritan woman's conversion.

The Man Born Blind (9:1-41)

John's dramatic skills reach a high point in this passage which is composed of seven scenes arranged in a concentric pattern below.[74] The length of the passage precludes reproducing it in its entirety, but we will highlight major emphases in each scene.

A. The Healing of the Man Born Blind (vv. 1–7)
 B. The Reaction (vv. 8–12)
  C. The First Interrogation (vv. 13–17)
   D. The Parents' Defense (vv. 18–23)
  C'. The Second Interrogation (vv. 24–34)
 B'. The Conversion to Faith (vv. 35–38)
A'. The Deeper Meaning Revealed (vv. 39–41)

The first scene establishes the setting and direction this conversion will take. Emphasis is on the external (and divine) cause of the man's blindness, for he is born that way. In place of the traditional explanation that either his sin or that of his parents caused the blindness, Jesus says, "Neither he nor his parents sinned; it is so that the works of God might be made *visible* through him" (v. 3). The cure of a man who cannot see will lead to others' new in*sight.* Two other themes we have seen previously come to the fore as well, namely, the contrast between night and day and Jesus as the light, and the water imagery associated with baptism. Jesus then "anoints" the man's eyes (cf. vv. 7 and 11) instructs him, "Go wash in the Pool of Siloam"; and he returns "able to *see*" (v. 7).

Scene two shows the resulting controversy among the man's neighbors, their disbelief that he can see, and the confusion over "where" Jesus, the healer, is. The first stage of the blind man's conversion is marked by his acknowledgement that "the man called Jesus" cured him (v. 11). This leads to an interrogation of the blind man by the Pharisees in scene three.

The third scene marks a further stage in the man's conversion. When he is angrily questioned, "What do you have to say about him [Jesus], since he opened your eyes?" his response is a deeper insight: "He is a prophet" (v. 17).

The fourth scene becomes pivotal. In an effort to find some explanation for this case, the Jewish leaders interrogate the blind man's parents. They, however, are reluctant to say anything for fear that they would be "expelled from the synagogue" (v. 22). So they put the responsibility for testimony in this case back onto their son, of whom they insist, "He is of age; question him" (v. 23). This turning back responsibility to the man's own testimony sharpens the challenge to the Jewish leaders not to resist but to believe.

This in turn leads to scene five and the second interrogation of the former blind man. With each scene more and more evidence mounts that the man is not only healed but truly converted. Rather than cowering at the leaders' threatening questions (like his parents did), he throws a startling question back to them: "Do you want to become his *disciples, too?*" (v. 27). He has tipped his hand and shown that he has indeed become a disciple of Jesus, as the leaders are quick to acknowledge (v. 28). He proceeds to mock their lack of knowledge about how to explain his cure, and the text simply says, "Then they threw him out" (v. 34). His conversion results in suffering, as indeed does discipleship (15:18).

The final two scenes are the climax of the story. Scene six describes the final stage of the man's conversion and his deepest confession of his faith in Jesus. The seventh scene provides a commentary on the importance of the entire story. At this point we will let the text speak for itself:

Scene Six

[35]When Jesus heard that they had thrown him out, he found him and said, "Do you *believe* in the Son of Man?" [36]He answered and said, "Who is he, sir, that I may believe in him?" [37]Jesus said to him, "You have *seen* him and the one speaking with you is he." [38]He said, *"I do believe, Lord,"* and he *worshiped* him (vv. 35–38).

Scene Seven

[39]Then Jesus said, "I came into this world for *judgment*, so that those who do not *see* might *see*, and those who do *see* might become *blind*." [40]Some of the Pharisees who were with him heard this and said to him, "Surely, we are not also *blind*, are we?" [41]Jesus said to them, "If you were *blind*, you would have no *sin;* but now you are saying, *'We see,'* so *your sin remains*" (vv. 39–41).

The story comes full circle, back to the question of who is truly blind and who can see. The focus is not only on the blind man's growth in faith, coming to the full acknowledgement of Jesus as Lord and being able to worship him. Rather, the story has broader implications in the realm of "judgment" (*krisis;* Löffler 1975: 37).[75] Conversion requires an existential decision or judgment either *for* or *against* Jesus (cf. John 3:19; 5:22; 12:31; 16:8). In this case, the blind man, who never disputes his lowly and sinful status, comes to faith in Jesus while the established leaders who deny their sinfulness prove themselves to be utterly blind to the truth before them. They who can literally "see" choose to walk in the dark and ignore the light, whereas the blind man responds to the "light" in his presence and leaves the darkness behind. True conversion can be described in no better terms.

Summary

Having explored several important passages in John, we are now in a position to extrapolate some general comments about how the Fourth Gospel views conversion. It offers a delectable feast for those who hunger for a different perspective.

1) The absence of traditional conversion language does *not* indicate a lack of interest in the topic. Rather, it signals that John views conversion through a unique optic that requires entering his cosmic worldview.

2) Some traditional imagery for conversion is used but in a much more developed way. This is especially the case with the movement from darkness to light, from blindness to sight. Though Acts shows an interest in these themes (and other basic conversion stories utilize them as well), John makes them prominently characteristic of conversion.

3) At the heart of conversion is the *personal encounter* with Jesus Christ. He who has been sent by his Father initiates the encounter. It is a revelation and a gift which demands a response (judgment). The goal of conversion is very christologically centered: to believe in Jesus Christ. This faith is an active, dynamic force which shows itself in concrete commitment to truth and to love.

4) John makes use of much sacramental imagery, especially baptism, but keeps it in the background. Baptism and the Spirit are essential components of conversion, but they do not become the object of conversion descriptions. Instead, a unique image is used, the necessity to be "born from above." In conversion one is invited to be transformed from earthly cares to heavenly cares by rebirth in the Spirit.

5) Perhaps most interesting is John's emphasis on conversion *in stages*. It is not a critical moment but a gradual process of growth and in*sight*. People can be at different stages on a continuum of growth and still be part of the new life of conversion.

6) Conversion will entail giving testimony to others but it will also lead to suffering and rejection by the world, because people all too often prefer the darkness over the light.

With John we come to the end of Gospel instruction on conversion. We now turn to the Letters of Paul.

7

Conversion in the Letters of Paul: Revelation from God

We have already examined the conversion of Paul in chapter four above, but it was only Luke's version in Acts 9; 22 and 26 which we considered. The task of this chapter is to explore what Paul says *in his own words* about his conversion and about Christian conversion in general.[76]

At the outset we already have a difficulty. The NT contains thirteen letters which have Paul's name attached to them. But scholars have determined that not all of them are genuinely from Paul's own hand. With the majority of scholars I accept seven letters as genuine.[77] The remaining six may or may not be genuine, in whole or in part, but most are considered "Deutero-Pauline," i.e., attributed to later writers who authored the letters in Paul's name.[78] This was a standard practice in antiquity. It lended authority to writings and also continued (with some refinements) an established tradition. Because these Deutero-Pauline letters at least have Paul's tradition as their starting point we will include discussion of them in the last section of this chapter.

The Genuine Letters of Paul

Paul's Conversion

It is rather startling to read Paul's letters and realize how seldom he makes reference to his own conversion experience. Unlike Acts, there is no dramatic narrative describing how Paul himself experienced the Damascus road conversion (and call). The event receives minimal attention, but when Paul does speak of it, it is clear that it was a major transformation in his life. The most prominent mention appears in Galatians 1:11-17:

> [11]Now I want you to know, brothers, that the gospel preached by me is not of human origin. [12]For I did not receive it from a human being, nor was I taught it, but it came through *a revelation of Jesus Christ.*
>
> [13]For you heard of my former way of life in Judaism, how I persecuted the church of God beyond measure and tried to destroy it, [14]and progressed in Judaism beyond many of my contemporaries among my race, since I was even more a zealot for my ancestral traditions. [15]But when [God], who from my mother's womb had *set me apart* and *called me through his grace,* was pleased [16]to *reveal his Son* to me, so that I might proclaim him to the Gentiles, I did not immediately consult flesh and blood, [17]nor did I go up to Jerusalem to those who were apostles before me; I went rather to Arabia and then returned to Damascus.

Paul mentions "Damascus," but gives us no description of what went on there. When we read this passage, we must keep in mind that it occurs in the context of Paul's vigorous defense of both his gospel (the message of Jesus Christ which he preaches) and his apostleship. He is at pains to insist that his ministry does not originate by means of *human* intervention. It is of *divine* origin, having come to him by "a revelation (*apokalypseōs*) of Jesus Christ." His double reference to a *revelation* in this passage (cf. also Gal 2:2) by means of a related noun and verb is the heart of his description of the Damascus road incident. No other explanation is offered. There is no "story" to go along with his description, though he also refers to the experience as a prophetic call (cf. Isa 49:1; Jer 1:5), a commissioning through God's grace to become an apostle to the Gentiles.

What does Paul mean by a "revelation of Jesus Christ"? Although the Greek allows for a subjective genitive (Jesus as the source) or an objective genitive (Jesus as the content), context favors the latter. But how did God "reveal" his Son to Paul? Unfortunately, the phrase itself does not yield a concrete description. It literally means an "unveiling," some sort of divine communication which transformed him from persecutor to proclaimer, but it does not tell us *how* Paul experienced this event from either a psychological or scientifically objective point of view. It seems to place the experience into a category of mystery, but not for purposes of obfuscation. The experience transcends the category of ecstasy, for it has eschatological dimensions in which Paul glimpses the kingdom to come (e.g. Rom 8:18-19; 1 Cor 3:13).

Paul also speaks of this event elsewhere with somewhat different language. In a significant passage on the resurrection of Jesus, he says:

> [8]Last of all, as to one born abnormally, he (Jesus) *appeared* to me. [9]For I am the least of the apostles, not fit to be called an apostle, because I persecuted the church of God. [10]But *by the grace of God* I am what I am, and *his grace* to me has not been ineffective. Indeed, I have toiled harder than all of them; not I however, but the *grace of God* [that is] with me (1 Cor 15:8-10).

Paul again defends his apostleship but strongly attributes it to God's grace (a threefold mention in one verse!). In this case, the word Paul uses instead of revelation is the verb, "appeared." The entire passage (vv. 1-11) concerns a series of appearances of the risen Lord to various apostles and disciples, the last of whom is Paul. Again, as with "reveal" or "revelation," the word has a certain imprecision to it. Although the word "appear" occurs in many passages about the risen Lord and implies a visionary rather than auditory experience, it does not describe how such an appearance is received. But Paul's meaning is clear. Despite his own prior record as a persecutor, he, no less than the other apostles, received by means of God's grace a personal appearance of the crucified and risen Lord which transformed his life.

Paul can be forgiven for what appears to be an act of hybris in his assertion that he works "harder than all of them," because he sometimes felt himself opposed and underappreciated by some of the other apostles (cf. Gal 2:1-14; 5:7-12; 2 Cor 11:5). He periodically lists the sufferings he has undergone for the sake of proclaiming the gospel of Jesus Christ (e.g., 2 Cor 11:21–30), but it is only so that he might "boast in the Lord" (2 Cor 10:17) and not exalt himself. The sufferings are an inherent part of conversion because they mediate the embrace of the cross of Jesus (1 Cor 1:23) as an essential part of Christian life.

Two other passages shed further light on Paul's experience. One is a description of "visions and revelations of the Lord" (2 Cor 12:1) which seems to be autobiographical:

> ²I know someone in Christ who, fourteen years ago (whether in the body or out of the body I do not know, God knows) was *caught up* to the third heaven. ³And I know that this person (whether in the body or out of the body I do not know, God knows) ⁴was *caught up* into Paradise and heard *ineffable things,* which no one may utter. ⁵About this person I will boast, but about myself I will not boast, except about my weaknesses. ⁶Although if I should wish to boast, I would not be foolish, for I would be telling the truth. But I refrain, so that no one may think more of me than what he sees in me or hears from me ⁷because of the *abundance of the revelations* (2 Cor 12:2–7a).

Paul again uses the language of revelation (in plural) and associates it with an ecstatic experience of finding oneself in heaven and becoming privy to divine mysteries which are otherwise kept secret (cf. similar language in Rom 16:25). Although Paul does not describe these revelations in detail, it is clear they come from God and are not part of his own spiritual achievement. The "revelations" bring him into direct contact with the divine mystery. The passage goes on to commend his sufferings as an apostle which have helped to keep him humble (2 Cor 12:7b–10), with the result that he boasts of his "weaknesses" rather than his privileges (2 Cor 11:30; 12:10).

Another passage indicates how important God's revelation has been in his life:

> ⁷[But] whatever gains I had [i.e., in Judaism], these I have come to consider a loss because of Christ. ⁸More than that, I even consider everything as a loss because of the supreme good of *knowing Christ Jesus my Lord.* For his sake I have accepted the loss of all things and I consider them so much *rubbish,* that

> I may *gain Christ* ⁹and be found in him, not having any *right-*
> *eousness* of my own based on the law but that which comes
> through *faith in Christ,* the *righteousness from God,* depend-
> ing on faith ¹⁰to *know* him and the power of his *resurrection*
> and [the] sharing of his sufferings by being conformed to his
> death, ¹¹if somehow I may attain the *resurrection* from the dead
> (Phil 3:7–11).

These words, too, occur in the context of an autobiographical
defense of his ministry (Phil 2:4b–6). He insists that though he
was as good as any Pharisaic Jew in observance of the law, he
counts his former life as "rubbish" (very strong language in the
Greek) compared to what he has gained in Jesus Christ. He contrasts the "righteousness" of the law with the "righteousness of
God," showing that the latter is infinitely superior. It has led to
"faith" in Christ, an intimate "knowledge" of the risen Lord,
and a share in the hope of resurrection. Both words, righteousness and faith, are key in Paul's thought and require a little explanation.

Righteousness (*dikaiosynē*) can also be translated "justification." In the past, Protestant interpreters tended to make "justification by faith alone" *the* key teaching in Paul, whereas Catholics
tended to see it as *a* central Pauline theme. Too often this distinction was fueled by an overly dichotomized understanding of
the difference between "faith" and "works" in Paul's thought.
Today there is a more moderate position among interpreters.
Justification is viewed as gift from God, but it shows itself concretely in good works. Paul insists that he has not *earned* this gift
(Rom 1:17; 3:21–22), but his life must bear the signs that he is
indeed justified by faith.⁷⁹

The word "faith" (*pistis* and the verb *pisteuein*) is also important in Paul. Coming to faith *in Christ* actually is a central expression for what Paul means by conversion (Löffler 1975: 36).
He views the entire conversion experience as an infusion of the
Christ event into one's life. It is almost a mystical expression,
describing a new way of living which comes about through baptism as one is baptized into Christ's own death in order to be born
anew (Rom 6:4, 8). Faith is that new relationship with God in
Jesus that allows one to be totally transformed. Paul places in
tandem the notion of turning to God and the transformation

which this entails: ". . .whenever a person *turns* (*epistrepsē*) to the Lord the veil is removed. . . . All of us, gazing with unveiled face on the glory of the Lord, are being *transformed* (*metamorphoumetha*) into the same image from glory to glory, as from the Lord who is the Spirit" (2 Cor 3:16, 18). Faith, then, produces a profound metamorphosis, a deep conversion into the image of God.

For Paul himself, he felt there was no turning back once the conversion experience "in Christ" was started. It is to be invited deeper into the mystery of God being revealed in Jesus Christ. It is an invitation too good to refuse!

If Paul mentions little explicitly about the Damascus road incident as we know it from Acts, it is not because he thought it insignificant. But the issue scholars still debate is what *role* it plays in the formation of his theology. Some scholars believe it is *the* formative experience which shaped all of Paul's thought, and others view it as one factor among many.[80] Whichever is the case, it can hardly be denied that it had major influence in Paul's life and thought. For our purposes, it is sufficient to see that it offers us another perspective on conversion, one that emphasizes the mysterious revelatory nature of the experience. We now turn to see how Paul applies this to Christians in general.

General Understanding of Conversion

With regard to the general notion of conversion, we see that Paul uses conventional language, though not with great frequency. He can describe conversion in standard OT prophetic fashion as turning *to* God *from* idols (1 Thess 1:9). He can also speak of the ethical need for *repentance* from "impurity, immorality, and licentiousness" (2 Cor 12:21; cf. also Rom 2:4 and 2 Cor 7:9–10), or he can use the word *epistrephō* to describe backsliding, reverting to earlier weaknesses (Gal 4:9). This latter notion is coupled with a return to former "slavery" (Gal 4:8–11) but Paul goes on to make the most of the image. He challenges his congregations to become a new kind of "slaves," slaves of Jesus Christ, which paradoxically leads to a new "freedom" (1 Cor 7:22; Gal 1:10). Those who are "bound" to Christ no longer need to worry about salvation or the minutiae of the law, for they live in the freedom of God's children (Gal 4:1–7).

Paul can also utilize standard OT references to conversion but in new contexts. Thus in Romans 11:26–27 Paul quotes Isaiah 59:20–21 in the context of explaining how Israel will be saved once the Gentiles are converted, for God's covenant is irrevocable:

> "The deliverer will come out of Zion,
>   he will *turn away* godlessness from Jacob;
> and this is my covenant with them
>   when I *take away their sins.*"

In this fashion, Paul is also aware of the effect of conversion as removing sin and mediating salvation.

Of all the images in Paul used to describe conversion, none is more inspiring than the image of "new creation." It is an image Paul explicitly connects with reconciliation in one of his most profound passages:

> [16]Consequently, from now on we regard no one according to the flesh; even if we once knew Christ according to the flesh, yet now we know him so no longer. [17]So whoever is *in Christ* is a *new creation; old things* have passed away; behold, *new things* have come. [18]And all this is *from God,* who has *reconciled* us to himself through Christ and given us the *ministry of reconciliation,* [19]namely, God was *reconciling* the world to himself in Christ, not counting their *trespasses* against them and entrusting to us the *message of reconciliation.* [20]So we are *ambassadors* for Christ, as if God were appealing through us. We implore you on behalf of Christ, *be reconciled to God.* [21]For our sake he made him to be sin who did not know sin, so that we might become the righteousness of God in him (2 Cor 5:16–21; cf. Gal 6:15).

These words are all the more poignant when one recalls that Paul had a stormy relationship with the Corinthian community. He felt great affection for them, yet he continually had to reprimand them and call them back to their Christian responsibilities (e.g., 1 Cor 5:1–2; 11:18). This passage elicits the tension in Paul's thought between the indicative and imperative mood. On the one hand, he states that the Corinthians *are reconciled* in Christ. On the other hand, he exhorts them to *be reconciled* to God. For Paul it is no paradox to say to people, "become what you are." Paul has no illusion that this newness is a once-and-for-all event. He acknowledges the *ongoing* nature of conversion by denying that he is perfect (Phil 3:12–14). Individual conversion entails communal responsibilities (Gaventa 1986: 45–46). It can never resort to business as usual. He makes it clear that conversion is not like putting a patch on old clothes. Rather, it is being clothed in a whole new garment. Conversion makes everything *new*. Incorporation *into* Christ changes the whole world by bringing reconciliation. Its effect is to make those who accept this reconciliation "ambassadors," personal representatives of Christ carrying forth the same message of reconciliation as intermediaries.

Many people who describe conversion experiences can identify with Paul's language of newness. That is a primary effect of conversion. The way one views the world, the way one lives, is dramatically changed and for the good. To utilize Paul's earlier reference to metamorphosis is entirely appropriate. This word aptly recalls the evolution of a caterpillar into a butterfly. It is change of the most dramatic kind. It is not just a new cloak thrown over an old body. The entire body is new. For Paul, such is human existence *in Christ* as a result of conversion.

One final note can be brought to bear on Paul's thought about conversion. He has a broad universalistic vision: conversion brings unity. He boldly states:

> There is neither Jew nor Greek, there is neither slave nor free person, there is not male and female; for you are all *one* in Christ Jesus (Gal 3:28; cf. 5:6; Rom 10:12; 1 Cor 12:13).

God's salvation is meant for all and has the ability to reconcile all so that differences melt into the background. Of course, Paul had to struggle often with his communities to get them to be more unified with one another. The tension between the ideal and the real was not eradicated by Paul's rhetoric. The Corinthian community especially was notorious for its factions (1 Cor 1:10–13). Nevertheless the communal dimension of conversion remains: it brings about a deeper unity among all who become part of "the body of Christ" (1 Cor 12:27).

The Deutero-Pauline Literature

The remaining six letters of the NT attributed to Paul do not say a great deal about conversion either in the conventional sense or using Paul's terminology. Occasionally passages hark back to specifically Pauline concepts. One example is Colossians 3:9–11 which refers to the newness that comes from Christian conversion and the unity that is found in Christ:

> ⁹Stop lying to one another, since you have taken off the *old self* with its practices ¹⁰and have put on the *new self,* which is being *renewed,* for knowledge, in the image of its creator. ¹¹Here there is not Greek and Jew, circumcision and uncircumcision, barbarian, Scythian, slave, free; Christ is all and in all.

This passage builds upon Paul's insight, yet the tone of the passage is different, reflecting Colossians' more "cosmic" christology.

Another reference to Pauline imagery is a reminder of the importance of baptism for the Christian: "You were buried with him in baptism, in which you were also raised with him through faith in the power of God, who raised him from the dead" (Col 2:12). On the whole, however, the Deutero-Pauline letters speak of other issues facing the Christian community, sometimes developing a seminal thought of Paul further (e.g., Christ as the *head* of the body, the Church; Eph 5:23; Col 1:18).

There are two primary examples of the development of the notion of conversion further in the Deutero-Pauline literature, one in Ephesians and one in the Pastoral Epistles.

Ephesians

The first example is found in an obscure passage which is notoriously difficult to translate:

> ⁸For you were once in *darkness,* but now you are *light* in the Lord. Live as *children of the light,* ⁹for *light* produces every kind of goodness and righteousness and truth. ¹⁰Try to learn what is pleasing to the Lord. ¹¹Take no part in the fruitless works of *darkness;* rather *expose* them, ¹²for it is shameful even to mention the things done by them in secret; ¹³but everything ex-

posed by the *light* becomes visible, [14]for everything that becomes visible is *light.* Therefore, it says:

> Awake, O sleeper,
>   and arise from the dead,
> and Christ will give you *light* (Eph 5:8–14).

The light and darkness contrast is, of course, more reminiscent of John's Gospel (3:20–21; cf. 1 Cor 4:5; Col 1:13) than it is of Paul. It is in any case associated with conversion. The crux of the interpretational problem is the verb "expose" (*elegchein*). Troels Engberg-Pedersen (1989) has recently offered a convincing interpretation which understands the passage to be about the *divided self.* Within a person there are things hidden in the heart (darkness) which require a confrontation so that they might come into the light (be exposed) and be changed. Conversion is thus the community's act of confrontation of an individual's inner self so that an effective change may occur.

How feasible is this interpretation? Certainly the notion of a divided self is consonant with a general theological understanding of conversion (e.g., St. Augustine's *Confessions*). It might also be considered at least in the background of Paul's thought (e.g., Rom 7:15–25).[81] And the movement from darkness to light is archetypical NT imagery for conversion. But I think support for Engberg-Pedersen's interpretation might even be found elsewhere in Ephesians:

> [14]For he [Christ] is our peace, he who made both one and broke down the *dividing wall* of enmity, through his flesh, [15]abolishing the law with its commandments and legal claims, that he might create in himself *one new person in place of the two,* thus establishing peace, [16]and might *reconcile* both to God, in one body, through the cross, putting that enmity to death by it (Eph 2:14–16).

The immediate context of this passage concerns unity between Israel and Gentiles which is found in Christ. The goal, as the author tells his readers, is to create one "household of God" with Christ as the "capstone" (Eph 2:19–20). But this is also a perfect description for what happens in Christ not only on the external, communal level, but also *internally.* Conversion (for example, from sin to grace) is the experience of the divided self being made whole again. It is creating a new person out of the building blocks of evil thoughts and deeds, and good thoughts and deeds, which exist in the human person. Conversion is thus reconciliation of the divided person in the new person of Christ.

The Pastoral Epistles

A second example of further development on conversion is in the Pastoral Epistles (1 and 2 Timothy; Titus). Traditional language of repentance is used but the object of that repentance is different. For the Pastorals the concern is less about turning from sin than it is protecting sound doctrine. The author of the Pastorals is concerned that some members of the community are straying from the truth, so he urges gentle but firm correction: "It may be that God will grant them *repentance* that leads to knowledge of the truth, and that they may return to their senses out of the devil's snare, where they are entrapped by him, for his will" (2 Tim 2:25b–26). This is expressed elsewhere in the fear that some "will stop listening to the truth and be diverted (*apostrepsousin*) to myths" (2 Tim 4:4; cf. Titus 1:14). For the Pastorals, then, straying from the truth of sound doctrine requires conversion, being brought back into the fold of correct beliefs.

Summary

Despite the fact that Paul is perhaps *the* most significant figure in the NT associated with conversion, he actually has comparatively little specific to say about the topic. We can summarize the testimony of Paul and the Pauline tradition in five statements.

1) The clearest language Paul himself uses is that his own conversion was a "revelation" from God, an "appearance" of the Risen Lord Jesus. This fact alone was sufficient for him to be known as an *apostle*,[82] one commissioned by the Lord himself to spread the gospel. This experience is part of the unveiling of the mystery of God, and it is a free gift God offers to those willing to embrace it.

2) Conversion is for the average Christian mediated through baptism which brings one to *faith*. It is the experience of being

"in Christ" and of being justified by faith alone. It leads to a life of proper ethical behavior which reflects this new state of faith.

3) The result of conversion is that one becomes totally a "new creation." Human divisions are reconciled in the conversion to Christ, and there is a universal call for all to become part of the "body of Christ." This personal experience of reconciliation leads to a ministry of inviting others to be reconciled to God in Christ.

4) In Ephesians, part of the Deutero-Pauline tradition, conversion is the healing of the divided inner self by means of the community's challenging individuals to move from *darkness* into *light*.

5) In the Pastoral Epistles, another part of the Deutero-Pauline tradition, conversion becomes doctrinally motivated. Straying from sound doctrine, from the truth that has been passed on in the community, requires repentance, coming back to the truth.

In conclusion, Paul and the tradition that carried on his name and his inspiration show multiple aspects of conversion which are uniquely developed and applied. To complete our survey of NT conversion, we will explore in the next chapter pertinent passages from the remaining NT books.

8

Conversion in Other
New Testament Books

This chapter will be of necessity a kind of *omnium gatherum.* The remaining references to conversion in the NT are infrequent and scattered, defying much synthesis. We will examine the particular NT books in their canonical order.

The Letter to the Hebrews

Designating Hebrews a "letter" is really a misnomer, for it only cursorily conforms to a letter's format. Instead it is an exhortatory written homily or a theological treatise which the unknown author terms "a message of encouragement" (13:22). The technical word *metanoia* occurs in three instances in two separate passages.

The first occurrence of the word "repentance" appears in the context of a passage exhorting the readers to spiritual growth and maturity:

> ¹Therefore, let us leave behind the basic teaching about Christ and *advance to maturity,* without laying the foundation all over again: *repentance* from dead works and faith in God, ²instruction about baptisms and laying on of hands, resurrection of the dead and eternal judgment. ³And we shall do this, if *only God permits.* ⁴For it is impossible in the case of those

who have once again been enlightened and *tasted* the heavenly
gift and shared in the holy Spirit 'and *tasted* the good word
of God and the powers of the age to come, 'and then have fallen
away, to bring them to *repentance again,* since they are
recrucifying the Son of God for themselves. . ." (Heb 6:1–6).

Context implies that the concern here is with apostates in the community who are turning from the faith. Two beautiful images are
employed which relate to faith. The first is the call to grow beyond the fundamentals of faith to spiritual maturity. The second
is the image of "tasting" the faith, i.e., coming to know it by
personal experience.

The dominant tone of the passage, however, is largely negative. It is indeed troubling for two reasons. One reason is the rigorous position of the impossibility of a second repentance. The
other reason is the striking image of the result of the apostates'
actions; they are crucifying Jesus all over again by their apostasy.
The sternness of the passage is strengthened by the threat of judgment which follows in verse 8. Utilizing the image of plants which
produce "thorns and thistles," the author insists that apostates
will be "cursed and finally burned." This negative image is reinforced by the second reference to repentance. Hebrews 12:17
brings to the fore the OT figure of Esau who sold his birthright
for a meal (Gen 27:34–38). Hebrews says that "he was rejected
because he found no opportunity to *change his mind. . . .*"
Thus, he is used as a negative example who illustrates the impossibility of multiple acts of repentance.

What are we to make of this stern view when compared to, for
instance, the Lukan perspective that there is always a possibility
of conversion, since repentance leads to God's forgiveness? Two
comments suffice for our purposes. First, it is important to note
that Hebrews, like the rest of the NT, acknowledges that *God*
alone is the one who brings people to spiritual maturity (Heb 6:3).
It is thus within God's power to "permit" spiritual growth through
repentance and consequently effect conversion. Second, the wider
context of Hebrews suggests a more hopeful exhortation to become spiritually mature. As Harold Attridge, a commentator who
places these words in their wider context, says, "While the rigorous attitude that our author represents lies behind the controver-

sies on the subject of repentance in the early church, he is not addressing systematically the problem of penitential discipline."[83] In this larger context the author of Hebrews is warning people of the serious consequences of backsliding in faith, but he still envisions a hopeful outcome. He concludes by exhorting the readers to be "imitators of those who, through faith and patience, are inheriting the promises" (Heb 6:12).

In brief, Hebrews takes a rigorous stance toward conversion as repentance, preferring to emphasize the importance of remaining faithful to baptismal promises and foundational Christian teaching. Yet it ultimately recognizes God's power to bring people to spiritual maturity. If it is impossible for those who deny their faith to turn again to God, Hebrews does not deny that God can turn again to them.

The Letter of James

This NT document is also mislabeled a "letter." It is more in the form of an exhortational treatise, sharply influenced by traditional OT motifs and filled with multiple ethical exhortations. In the midst of imploring the readers to correct ethical conduct comes a remarkably hope-filled statement about the possibility of conversion:

> [19]My brothers, if anyone among you should *stray from the truth* and someone *bring him back* (*epistrepsē*), [20]he should know that whoever brings back a *sinner* from the error of his way will *save* his soul from death and will cover a multitude of sins (James 5:19–20).

One could hardly find a more positive image in contrast to the stern negative image we just examined in Hebrews. Two aspects of this passage call for comment.

One noteworthy item is the implication that conversion is an *internally* directed activity within the community. Members of the community bear responsibility for one another to "bring back" those who stray. Communal outreach is an essential aspect of conversion. Another interesting notion comes from the deliberate ambiguity of verse 20, even as it comes across in English. Not only does the sinner have his or her sins forgiven in the process of conversion, but the verse can be read to include the one who mediates the conversion as a recipient of salvation as well.[84] Communal responsibility for one another in conversion thus results in mutual salvation.

In contrast to Hebrews, then, James has a more positive image of ongoing Christian conversion.

The Letters of 1 and 2 Peter

These later NT period letters contain only minor mention of conversion. We will consider them separately because scholars see them as unrelated pseudonymous documents (i.e., written by anonymous authors writing in Peter's name).

Scholars disagree whether the First Letter of Peter is actually a letter. Some consider it a moral exhortation and others a baptismal homily. In any case, baptismal, creedal, and liturgical imagery abound. The beginning of the letter commends Christian *"new birth* to a living hope through the resurrection of Christ from the dead. . ."* (1 Pet 1:3). While the expression in Greek is neither Paul's "new creation" nor the Gospel of John's "born-from-above," nevertheless the main thrust of the letter is on the *new life* Christians obtain in Christ by means of baptism. The letter goes on to commend the forgiveness of sins which Jesus' crucifixion has achieved:

> [24]He himself bore our sins in his body upon the cross, so that free from sin, we might live for righteousness. By his wounds you have been healed. [25]For you had *gone astray* like sheep, but you have now *returned* (*epestraphēte*) to the shepherd and guardian of your souls (1 Pet 2:24–25).

This imagery evokes other NT passages where the experience of sinfulness and conversion is described as going astray like sheep and returning to the shepherd (Matt 18:10–14; Luke 15:4–7). This document simply builds upon other NT imagery but places conversion in a distinctive context of instruction toward proper ethical behavior.

The Second Letter of Peter is probably the latest book in the NT, written in the early second century in Peter's name, and differing in character and content from 1 Peter. It includes one general comment on repentance in the context of concern over the delay of the parousia, Christ's second coming. "The Lord does not delay his promise, as some regard 'delay,' but he is patient with you, not wishing that any should perish but that all should come to repentance (*metanoian*)" (2 Pet 3:9). The specific character of conversion as repentance is never defined by 2 Peter, but controversy over false teachers and over preparedness for the second coming of Christ and its concomitant day of judgment would reinforce the image we have seen earlier in an eschatological context (e.g., as in Matthew). Repentance is necessary to avoid judgment. And God will patiently deal with those who truly repent because God is patient and does not desire sinners' destruction.

In summary, 1 and 2 Peter give evidence of the rather standard view of conversion we have seen earlier in the Synoptic Gospels. There is little distinctive about the character of repentance except in the larger context of late NT period concerns which are beyond the scope of this book.

The Book of Revelation

The final book of the NT interestingly brings us full circle in our discussion of conversion. Not only is frequent reference made to conversion (the verb, *metanoeō* twelve times!), but it is used exhortationally in the context of coming eschatological judgment.

Contemporary understanding of the Book of Revelation is unfortunately marred by the general public's failure to recognize the symbolic nature of this literature. Far from being a blueprint for the "end of the world" in the last decade of the twentieth century, Revelation is a book of *hope* offered to persecuted Christians of the late first century A.D. Contrary to spreading the message of doom and gloom which many a TV evangelist would have us believe, Revelation is a book offering assurance that Christ is ultimately the victor over evil. The form of the message is in a series of visions which John of Patmos (otherwise unknown in the NT) receives. The basic message is that no matter how bad things might look, Christ's victory over evil and sin is assured. Faithful Christians who persevere will be part of the "saints" who go marching into the kingdom of heaven. How does the message of conversion fit into this scenario?

Revelation uses the verb "repent" in three basic ways. Sometimes the word is used in a simple statement that some people (according to John's vision) failed to "repent" from idolatry and other sins (2:21; 9:20, 21; 16:9, 11). At other times, the verb is attached conditionally to a warning about some impending judgmental action which will be taken "unless you repent" (2:5, 22). But the most potent use of the verb is in the imperative sense of a strong exhortation, "Repent!" (2:5, 16; 3:3, 19). These latter references are in the context of symbolic letters written to the seven churches in Asia Minor (1:4—3:22). The Greek tense (aorist imperative) in this context indicates that this call to conversion is not a plea to maintain currently ongoing Christian conversion but a sharp, powerful challenge to be converted now. Conversion must finally begin! The exhortation is given in the spirit of the need for watchfulness, for the day of judgment can come at a moment's notice (Rev 3:3).

Revelation thus emphasizes conversion in the sense of repentance as a human action, turning away from sinfulness. It is coupled with the plea to be patient and faithful in the face of peril and the promise that it will result in participation of a "new heaven and new earth" (21:1) which God will establish in the coming kingdom. This newness is carried over into the image of a heavenly city, the "new Jerusalem" (21:2) which will be the dwelling place of all those who have been purified by "the blood of the Lamb" (7:14). Although repentance is the human action of turning away from sin and back to God's ways, Revelation equally emphasizes that the soteriological effect of conversion is from God alone. "*Salvation* comes from our God, who is seated on the throne, and from the Lamb" (7:10). Christ's own sacrifice achieves the salvation which conversion envisions, and his sacrifice in turn gives us hope to endure the sufferings which come our way in this world.

Revelation's vision of conversion brings us back to that contained in the Synoptic Gospels, especially Mark and Matthew. Conversion is a verb; it requires action. It is eschatologically flavored, challenging to the core, and an exhortation which must finally be heeded. But it is also coupled with a promise of salvation. Conversion never leaves us where we are, but takes us to a place that is entirely new. That promise and vision which Jesus offered at the beginning of the NT is also offered at the end: Repent, and believe the good news!

Summary

While it is not possible to synthesize these diverse passages on conversion into a unified whole, it is helpful to note that the rest of the NT offers a combination of the familiar and yet a nuanced understanding of this basic Christian message. These latter books take their cues from other NT materials and apply them to their distinctive situations. That is indeed how the message of conversion has survived to our own day. Our task now is to understand it in our own context.

9

A Biblical Theology of Conversion

The purpose of this final chapter is to pull together the scattered strands of biblical teaching on conversion into a coherent pattern. This is not an attempt to speak the final word on the nature of conversion. Our study has been more restricted. We have not incorporated insights from anthropological, psychological, and sociological studies, nor have we recorded the testimony of great historical figures of conversion, such as Augustine, John Henry Newman, Dorothy Day, or Edith Stein. Instead we have explored the biblical foundations of conversion, especially in the NT. We have tried to let the Bible speak on its own terms, so that we could discern what it says and does not say about this basic Christian notion. As a final synthesis of this biblical data, I offer fifteen statements which characterize the Bible's understanding of conversion.

Characteristics of Biblical Conversion

1) The Bible is quite consistent that conversion is primarily an *act of God*. It occurs at divine initiative. It is an experience of God's grace. Human beings interact with this grace and are called to respond to it, but they do not make it happen. It is a gift of the Holy Spirit who facilitates a change in life.

2) In keeping with all of God's activity, conversion entails an element of *mystery*. It is an intensely spiritual experience which

defies total analysis or rational explanation. It is difficult to describe and consequently requires reliance upon metaphor and symbol. For this reason, the NT often goes beyond the technical language of conversion into the realm of image.

3) Because of its complexity, conversion is related to a variety of other *biblical themes*. Among the most important are: sin, forgiveness, repentance, salvation, justification, baptism, faith, and the Holy Spirit. The total picture of conversion is reflected in the larger process of sanctification and salvation of a people. Conversion ultimately creates a new people of God.

4) The root notion of conversion in the Bible is change. It involves *turning* from sin, death, and darkness to grace, new life, and light. The dual action of turning always leads a person to a new level of human existence. It leads people together to spiritual maturity which is reflected in their abhorrence of evil and their attraction to good.

5) For the NT especially, conversion is directly related to the revelation of *the kingdom of God*. As such it is an eschatological reality, a foretaste of the new life which is to come. It is a final call issued to people to conform their lives to the values of the kingdom which is to come.

6) An aspect of conversion unique to the NT is that it is intimately tied to the person of Jesus Christ, in whom the kingdom is brought to fulfillment. Conversion is a *christological* reality. It is incorporation into the body of Christ and an intimate personal knowledge of Jesus Christ as Risen Lord and Savior.

7) Although conversion is an individual experience, the biblical understanding is that it is always *relational*. This relationality is bi-directional, being both vertical and horizontal. Conversion brings one into a new relationship with God and with other human beings. In the OT the covenant relationship with God is essential, and in the NT the relationship with Jesus Christ is primary. But both of these lead to new human interrelationships with responsibilities and privileges in the context of community. In light of this aspect, one can also perceive that the biblical call to conversion is properly directed to whole communities and not merely to individuals.

8) As regards community, the Bible's notion of conversion is both *externally* and *internally* directed. Although an aspect of con-

version is outwardly directed to bringing new people into the community of the church (evangelization), the lion's share of the NT message of conversion is directed to those who are already members of the believing community. Disciples no less than pagans need to hear the message of conversion.

9) The Bible indicates that there are different types of conversion. Some conversions are dramatic, single events which profoundly change a person's direction in life. But most conversions appear to be a *process* on some line of continuum. The message for disciples is that it is an ongoing process, a journey of faith, that requires consistent attention.

10) Although conversions happen at God's instigation, they also require *preparation*. Just as soil needs to be fertilized and watered for plants to be fruitful, so people who seek ongoing conversion in life need to be prepared for God's grace. Most frequently, the Bible singles out two aspects of preparation. The first is the recognition and explicit acknowledgement of sinfulness. One can only turn to God when one concomitantly turns away from sin. The second aspect is the necessity of hearing the word of God. Hearing is also an act of obedience (in Hebrew the word is the same!), and this also prepares one for conversion (Smalley 1964: 205-6).

11) Conversion always leads to an experience of *newness*. Even in cases of the rediscovery of a lost faith or the revitalization of a dead faith, conversion leads to some form of rebirth. Paul's language of "new creation" and John's language of "born again (from above)" sum up this image best. Ongoing Christian conversion involves the continual revitalization of faith. A good contemporary image might be that of a television commercial for a popular cereal that urges people to "taste them again for the first time"! Corny as it sounds, it expresses well what one accomplishes in Christian conversion. It is like a rediscovery of a lost precious item, or the rekindling of an old friendship, which leaves one refreshed and renewed.

12) Although the Bible cannot make the kinds of modern distinctions about human personality that psychology can, nevertheless the Bible's understanding of conversion is that it affects the *whole person*. It is not restricted to intellect, to morality, or even to spirituality. As an experience of God's grace, conversion in-

volves the mind, the body, the heart, and the spirit. It is the holistic action of God's love which sanctifies the whole person.

13) Conversion involves both *internal* (attitudinal) and *external* (behavioral) changes in life. Authentic Christian conversion is never divorced from concrete actions which mirror the changed internal reality. Conversion thus always leads to some aspect of social responsibility and justice.[85]

14) Conversion is also accompanied by concrete *symbolic gestures*. In the OT it is the renewal of the covenant or a cleansing water ritual which symbolizes the change, while in the NT baptism is the hallmark of Christian conversion. Conversion needs to be ritualized to be appreciated fully. This ritualization also provides a means for the total community to participate in the action by way of affirmation.

15) One prominent effect of conversion is the urge to give *testimony* to others and consequently to evangelize. Because conversion is so often a profound existential change in life, it is natural for people to have the urge to spread the "good news." Indeed, Jesus' message of salvation for all requires carrying the message forth to the ends of the earth (e.g., Matt 28:16–20; Acts 2:37–39). Evangelization is definitely an outcome of conversion but it must be seen in the proper perspective of the total message of ongoing conversion to all.

These fifteen statements summarize the basic components of NT conversion. They offer a vision of the dramatic transformation which God's grace can accomplish in human life. Conversion is indeed central to the message of Jesus. It proffers a remarkable process of change that leaves its impact on every aspect of human existence. Hulsbosch states succinctly the miracle that undergirds Christian conversion: "This is conversion as presented in salvation history surveyed in its totality: Jesus has made an idolatrous generation the holy people of God" (1966: 101).

The Role of Conversion in the Life of the Church

We have surveyed the information in the NT with regard to conversion and have found that, though it is not an extensively treated subject, it is central to Jesus' teaching and encompasses a broad spectrum of themes. To round out our exploration, one brief task remains—to point the direction toward the future. What does any of this have to do with the life of the contemporary church?

In the introduction we noted that conversion was a modern problem. In reality, it is not conversion which is the problem but our restricted way of understanding it. I want to return to a comment about conversion by Flannery O'Connor to help us focus some final remarks. In her collected letters she speaks of the role of conversion in her own life in a manner consistent with the NT perspective we have offered, and which can serve as a model of conversion in the life of the church. She writes:

> I don't think of conversion as being once and for all and that's that. I think once the process is begun and continues that you are continually turning inward toward God and away from your own egocentricity and that you have to see this selfish side of yourself in order to turn away from it. I measure God by everything that I am not. I begin with that.[86]

Continually turning toward God is what conversion is all about. In fact, it is about God continually turning toward us and calling us to return to a covenantal relationship. The Bible as the word of God is foundational for the life of the church. One of the ways in which the church has used the biblical teaching of conversion, and must continue to use it, is to direct it toward itself. This is a feature of Vatican II which I fear is overlooked when Catholics speak of conversion.

Vatican II made several striking references to the need for ongoing conversion in the life of the church. This idea is imbedded in the very notion of a "pilgrim church" on a journey to the kingdom, ever in need of renewal.[87] *Lumen gentium,* the "Constitution on the Church," refers to ongoing conversion in these words:

> [T]he church, containing sinners in its own bosom, is at one and the same time holy and always in need of purification and it pursues increasingly penance and renewal . . . under the action of the holy Spirit, it does not cease from renewing itself

> until, through the cross, it arrives at the light which knows no
> setting (*Lumen gentium* #8 and #9).[88]

These words indicate that Vatican II issued a clear call for the
church to heed the message of conversion for itself, even as it
urged an increase in evangelization to the world. Perhaps the most
striking expression of all is found in the "Decree on Ecumenism"
where reference is made twice to the need for ongoing "reformation." In general terms the document speaks of the church as a
unified whole:

> In its pilgrimage on earth Christ summons the church to con-
> tinual reformation (*perennem reformationem*), of which it is
> always in need, in so far as it is an institution of human beings
> here on earth (#6).

The document also spells out the duties of Catholic Christians
in specific terms:

> All Catholics must therefore aim at christian perfection
> [*perfectionem christianam*] and, each according to their situa-
> tion, play their part that the church, bearing in her own body
> the lowly and dying state of Jesus, may be daily more purified
> and renewed, against the day when Christ will present her to
> himself in all her glory without spot or wrinkle (#4).[89]

Given the history of Christendom's great split of the 16th century in the Protestant Reformation, these are sharp words which
sound a clarion call to hear Jesus' message of conversion over
and over again. Specific reference to ongoing "reformation" provides an antidote to Christian elitism, which is the singlemost opponent to effective conversion in contemporary life. This view
of conversion is not to deny the need for evangelization in the
life of the church. Evangelization is also part of Jesus' call to conversion and to discipleship. But too many of us Christians think
we have "made it." We've reached our goal, there is little more
to be done. The NT calls all Christians to heed the message of
ongoing personal and ecclesial renewal. The vision of Vatican II
is an acknowledgement that we as church remain sinners even
though the death and resurrection of Jesus has already assured

our salvation. The task of the future is to remind ourselves frequently of the need to hear Jesus' call to conversion afresh. Conversion is still that central call of Jesus: "Repent, and believe the good news!" The task of the future is like that reflected in the NT itself: to admit that these are words for all time.

Selected Bibliography

Baillie, John
1964   *Baptism and Conversion.* London: Oxford University.
            This short book discusses many aspects of conversion in a series of lectures originally given in 1955.

Beasley-Murray, George R.
1963   *Baptism in the New Testament.* London: Macmillan.
            The basic scholarly treatment of the topic of baptism in the NT. This book concludes that baptism and conversion are inseparable.

Bible Today, The 30:2
1992   The entire issue is devoted to conversion and provides a good but very brief introduction to the topic, with articles by I. Nowell, D. Launderville, M. T. McHatten, and S. A. Sharkey.

Cazelles, Henri
1989   "La notion de *'shub'* dans l'Ancien Testament," pp. 19–35 in Achille M. Triacca and Allesandro Pistoia (eds.), *Liturgie, Conversion et Vie Monastique.* Bibliotheca Ephemerides Liturgicae Subsidia 48; Rome: C.L.V.—Edizioni Liturgiche.
            A good summary of the OT data on conversion.

Cothenet, Edouard
1989   "La Conversion dans le IVe Évangile," pp. 55–71 in Achille M. Triacca and Allesandro Pistoia (eds.),

Liturgie, Conversion et Vie Monastique. Bibliotheca Ephemerides Liturgicae Subsidia 48; Rome: C.L.V.—Edizioni Liturgiche.
A helpful but incomplete survey of the Johannine concept of conversion.

Crosby, Michael H.
1987
"The Biblical Vision of Conversion," pp. 31–74 in Francis A. Eigo (ed.), *The Human Experience of Conversion: Persons and Structures in Transformation.* Villanova: Villanova University.
A lengthy treatment of the OT data on conversion, relying heavily on the earlier work of W. L. Holladay. A second section analyzes conversion in the Gospel of Matthew from a social justice perspective.

Dick, Michael Brennan
1984
"Conversion in the Bible," pp. 43–63 in Robert Duggan (ed.), *Conversion and the Catechumenate.* New York: Paulist.
A good introductory essay, intended for general audiences to summarize the biblical data on conversion.

Dupont, Jacques
1979
"Conversion in the Acts of the Apostles," pp. 61–84 in *The Salvation of the Gentiles.* New York: Paulist.
A classic essay from an expert on Acts. The entire book offers good insights into Luke-Acts.

Engberg-Pedersen, Troels
1989
"Ephesians 5,12–13: *elegchein* and Conversion in the New Testament," *Zeitschrift für die Neutestamentliche Wissenschaft* 80: 89–110.
A technical article intended for scholars, but it offers a precise study of one verb associated with some passages on conversion in the NT.

Fretheim, Terence E.
1988
"The Repentance of God: A Key to Evaluating Old Testament God-Talk," *Horizons in Biblical Theology* 10:47–70.
An excellent summary of this neglected OT theme.

Gaventa, Beverly Roberts
1986   *From Darkness to Light: Aspects of Conversion
                in the New Testament.* Philadelphia: Fortress.
                An interesting and insightful book which analyzes
                Paul's conversion from the individual perspective
                of Acts and his own letters, and conversion imagery
                in the Gospel of John and 1 Peter.

Heikkinen, J. W.
1967   "Notes on *'epistrepho'* and *'metanoeo,'* " *Ecumen-
                ical Review* 19: 313–16.
                A succinct treatment of these two primary NT verbs
                for conversion.

Holladay, William L.
1958   *The Root Šûbh in the Old Testament with Partic-
                ular Reference to Its Usage in Covenantal Contexts.*
                Leiden: E. J. Brill.
                The seminal study of conversion in the OT to which
                everyone refers. This is a technical work for schol-
                ars, but it offers an important analysis of the pro-
                phetic teaching on conversion.

Hulsbosch, A.
1966   *The Bible on Conversion.* De Pere, Wis.: St. Nor-
                bert Abbey.
                The primary monograph on a popular level on the
                broad topic of conversion in the Bible. Originally
                published in Dutch in 1963, this tiny book treats
                the OT background, Synoptic Gospels (together),
                and Acts. It also contains a final chapter on the
                biblical "theology" of conversion.

Lacan, Marc-François
1978   "Conversion and Grace in the Old Testament," pp.
                75–96 in Walter E. Conn (ed.), *Conversion: Per-
                spectives on Personal And Social Transformation.*
                New York: Alba House.

1978a   "Conversion and Kingdom in the Synoptic
                Gospels," pp. 97–118 in Walter E. Conn (ed.),
                Conversion.
                Both of these articles offer good popular sum-
                maries of a wealth of biblical material on con-
                version.

Leroy, Herbert
1972   "Wege der Bekehrung nach dem Neuen Testament," pp. 44–52 in Wilhelm Zauner and Helmut Erharter (eds.), *Freiheit - Schuld - Vergebung.* Vienna: Herder.
A good analysis of the teaching of John the Baptist and Jesus on conversion; emphasizes Jesus' unique way of connecting his own person with conversion.

Löffler, Paul
1965   "The Biblical Concept of Conversion," *Study Encounter* 1: 93–101.

1975   "The Biblical Concept of Conversion," pp. 24–45 in Gerald H. Anderson and Thomas F. Stransky (eds.), *Mission Trends No. 2—Evangelization.* New York: Paulist.
Two fine articles analyzing the biblical data especially for their implications for Christian missionary activity.

Michiels, R.
1965   "La conception lucanienne de la conversion," *ETL* 41: 42–78.
In conjunction with Dupont's work, this article offers an authoritative summary of the Lukan concept of conversion.

Nock, Arthur Darby
1969   *Conversion: The Old and New in Religion from Alexander the Great to Augustine of Hippo.* London: Oxford University.
A classic on conversion originally published in 1933. Its NT information is dated, but the perspective is always enriching. It offers a good summary of comparative religion data.

Rambo, Lewis R.
1982   "Current Research on Religious Conversion," *RelSRev* 8: 146–59.
Offers both a summary and an extensive bibliography on the general topic of conversion, including psychological, anthropological, and sociological studies.

Schmidt, Henry J. (ed.)

1980　　　　*Conversion: Doorway to Discipleship.* Hillsboro, Kans.: Board of Christian Literature of the General Conference of Mennonite Brethren Churches. An excellent collection of essays by various Mennonite scholars on diverse aspects of Christian conversion, built upon but going beyond the biblical data.

Sievernich, Michael

1983　　　　"Die christliche Auffassung von Schuld und Umkehr," pp. 19–42 in Michael Sievernich and Klaus Philipp Seif (eds.), *Schuld und Umkehr in den Weltreligionen.* Mainz: Matthias-Grünewald. As part of a comparative religion study this essay emphasizes the bi-directional nature of conversion, toward God and toward human beings.

Simian-Yofre, H.

1986　　　　*"nḥm,"* pp. 366–384 in G. J. Botterweck, H. Ringgren, and H.-J. Fabry (eds.), *Theologisches Wörterbuch zum Alten Testament.* Stuttgart: W. Kohlhammer. A technical study of this Hebrew verb. This should appear soon in English in a volume of the *Theological Dictionary of the Old Testament* (Grand Rapids: Eerdmans).

Sklba, Richard J.

1981　　　　"The Call to New Beginnings, A Biblical Theology of Conversion," *Biblical Theology Bulletin* 11: 67–73. A good, succinct summary of the OT notion of conversion intended for general audiences.

Smalley, Stephen

1964　　　　"Conversion in the New Testament," *The Churchman* 78: 193–210. A very good analysis of the NT data based upon the linguistic evidence but going beyond it to a helpful synthesis of the topic.

Trilling, Wolfgang

1965　　　　"Metanoia als Grundforderung der Neutestamentlichen Lebenslehre," pp. 178–90 in *Einübung des Glaubens.* FS Klemens Tilman; Würzburg: Echter.

A good synthetic theological treatment of the NT teaching on conversion. Trilling argues that, despite the dearth of conversion language, it is foundational to Christian faith.

Endnotes

[1]For a view of how these programs relate to the biblical notion of conversion, see Ronald D. Witherup, "Twelve Step Recovery and the Biblical Notion of Conversion," *Journal of Spiritual Formation,* forthcoming.

[2]For example, Luke Timothy Johnson, *The Writings of the New Testament: An Interpretation* (Philadelphia: Fortress, 1986); and *The New Jerome Biblical Commentary* (Englewood-Cliffs, N.J.: Prentice-Hall, 1990).

[3]*The American Heritage Dictionary,* 2nd college ed. (Boston: Houghton Mifflin, 1991) 320.

[4]"To William Dean Howells," in *The Portable Mark Twain* (ed., Bernard De Voto; New York: Penguin, 1977) 767.

[5]Donald Gelpi, "Religious Conversion: A New Way of Being," in Eigo (1987: 175-202) listed in the bibliography.

[6]Robert Duggan, *Conversion and the Catechumenate* (New York: Paulist, 1984) 122-25.

[7]For example, Alfred Clair Underwood, *Conversion: Christian and Non-Christian* (London: George Allen & Unwin, 1925); William James, *The Varieties of Religious Experience* (Garden City, N.Y.: Doubleday, 1978; original 1902); and Bernard J. F. Lonergan, *Method in Theology* (New York: Herder and Herder, 1972) 118, 130-31, 235-44.

[8]Quoted in Jill P. Baumgaertner, *Flannery O'Connor: A Proper Scaring* (Wheaton, Ill.: Harold Shaw, 1988) 2.

[9]A useful in-depth study of the prophetic notion of conversion is still Hans W. Wolff, "Das Thema 'Umkehr' in der alttestamentlichen Prophetie," *ZTK* 48 (1951) 129-48.

[10]The OT is not uniform in this perspective. Other covenants, e.g., the Davidic covenant (2 Sam 7:8-17), are unilateral (Dick 1984: 46-47).

[11]Hans Kasdorf (in Schmidt 1980: 20) indicates that *nḥm* means emotional and moral change whereas *shûb* refers to the physical sense of turning. But Cazelles (1989: 21) rightly notes that the two verbs, though not entirely interchangeable, occur several times in parallel and that both apply to true conversion.

[12]Lacan (1978: 76-79), with some justification, proposes David as the archetypical model of conversion in the OT.

[13]This proposal is most associated with George A. Mendenhall and Norman K. Gottwald. See the discussion in Crosby 1987: 34-34 and Cazelles 1989: 22-23. For a critique of this position, see Jacob Milgrom, "Religious Conversion and the Revolt Model for the Formation of Israel," *JBL* 101 (1982) 169-76.

[14]A direct implication found in the NT is in connection with prayer. Jesus encourages his disciples to "ask and you shall receive" precisely because God hears and responds to prayers of petition (e.g., Matt 7:7-11; Luke 11:5-13). It is a way of saying that our needs have an effect on (but do not control) God's intentions.

[15]Translation from John J. Collins in *The Old Testament Pseudepigrapha,* Vol. 1 (ed. James H. Charlesworth; Garden City, N.Y.: Doubleday, 1983) 388.

[16]Translation from Michael A. Knibb, *The Qumran Community* (Cambridge: Cambridge University, 1987) 90-91. For a fuller treatment of conversion and baptismal rituals at Qumran, see Joseph A. Fitzmyer, *Essays on the Semitic Background of the New Testament* (Missoula: Scholars' Press, 1974) 469-73; and Yves Fauquet, "La conversion dans la communauté de Qumrân," 105 22 in A. M. Triacca & A. Pistoia (eds.), *Liturgie, Conversion et Vie Monastique,* listed in the bibliography.

[17]The tense of the verb varies (usually present or aorist), but one must be cautious about interpreting meaning on the basis of tense alone. More important than tense is the context of each individual passage. See Stanley E. Porter, *Verbal Aspect in the Greek of the New Testament with Reference to Tense and Mood* (Studies in Biblical Greek #1; New York: Peter Lang, 1989) 351-60.

[18]For example, Paul W. Hollenbach, "The Conversion of Jesus: From Jesus the Baptizer to Jesus the Healer," *Aufstieg und Niedergang der Römischen Welt,* II.25.1 (ed. Wolfgang Haase; Berlin: W. De Gruyter, 1982) 196-219.

[19]Rudolf Pesch, *Das Markusevangelium,* Vol. I, 4th ed. (Freiburg: Herder, 1984) 94, against Joachim Jeremias and others.

[20]Porter, *Verbal Aspect,* 354.

[21] For more complete studies on discipleship in Mark see Ernest Best, *Disciples and Discipleship: Studies in the Gospel according to Mark* (Edinburgh: T. & T. Clark, 1986) and C. Clifton Black, *The Disciples according to Mark* (JSNTSup 27; Sheffield: JSOT, 1989).

[22] Mark's language of "following" Jesus here does not make Bartimaeus a literal disciple. Rather, Bartimaeus is used as an ironic "foil" to point out the failure of Jesus' own disciples.

[23] See especially, Theodore J. Weeden, Sr., *Mark - Traditions in Conflict* (Philadelphia: Fortress, 1971) and Werner H. Kelber, *Mark's Story of Jesus* (Philadelphia: Fortress, 1979).

[24] The use of the dual expression of reading/hearing reminds us that the Gospels originate in the oral proclamation of the early kerygma. See especially, Werner H. Kelber, *The Oral and Written Gospel* (Philadelphia: Fortress, 1983).

[25] Note Matthew's characteristic way of speaking of "the kingdom of God" with the paraphrastic "kingdom of heaven" (literally, "of the heavens"). This is one example of Matthew's Jewish style of expression. With the majority of scholars, I hold Matthew to be written by a Jewish-Christian of the late first century A.D. For a different opinion emphasizing the Gentile characteristics of this Gospel, see John P. Meier, *The Vision of Matthew* (New York: Paulist, 1979).

[26] The notion of "fruit" might originally have been a concept in Q, the hypothetical sayings document considered by most scholars as one of the key sources of the Synoptic Gospels (cf. Matt 3:8-9; Luke 3:8-9; and Matt 7:16-17; Luke 6:43-44). If so, Matthew nonetheless makes a major metaphor of it while Luke does not develop the concept.

[27] For a thorough study of this parable, see Klyne Snodgrass, *The Parable of the Wicked Tenants* (WUNT 27; Tübingen: J. C. B. Mohr [Paul Siebeck] 1983).

[28] Matthew 21:23 indicates the audience consists of "the chief priests and elders of the people" whereas 21:45 points to "the chief priests and the Pharisees." Though these are inconsistent, the Jewish leadership is clearly envisioned as the audience.

[29] Scholars are divided over whether this parable refers to the general treatment of those in need or concerns only the treatment of disciples of Jesus. See John R. Donahue, "The Parable of the Sheep and the Goats," *TS* 47 (1986) 3-31; and Sherman W. Gray, *The Least of My Brothers—Matthew 25:31-46—A History of Interpretation* (SBLDS 114; Atlanta: Scholars, 1989).

[30] Matthew's view of judgment must be tempered with his view of forgiveness. See Thomas W. Buckley, *Seventy Times Seven: Sin, judgment and forgiveness in Matthew* (Zacchaeus Studies; Collegeville: Liturgical, 1991).

[31]Matthew has a penchant for using vocabulary of humility and meekness with regard to Jesus and the disciples. See, for example, 5:5; 11:29; 21:5; 23:11-12.

[32]For more on the christology of Matthew's Gospel, see Jack Dean Kingsbury, *Matthew as Story*, 2nd ed. (Philadelphia: Fortress, 1988).

[33]The major study of this concept is Benno Przybylski, *Righteousness in Matthew and His World of Thought* (Cambridge: Cambridge University, 1980).

[34]For example, Otto Michel, *TDNT* IV, 628.

[35]*The New Jerusalem Bible* (Garden City, N.Y.: Doubleday, 1985) and *The Revised English Bible* (Oxford University and Cambridge University, 1989). Contrast the *New Revised Standard Version* (New York: Oxford University, 1989) which translates 27:3 with the words, "he repented."

[36]John P. Heil ("The Blood of Jesus in Matthew: A Narrative-Critical Perspective," *Perspectives in Religious Studies* 18 [1991] 117-24) proposes a similar interpretation of Judas' repentance but fails to note its negative function as a counter model of conversion.

[37]For example, Robert C. Tannehill, *The Narrative Unity of Luke-Acts,* 2 vols. (Foundations and Facets; Minneapolis: Fortress, 1986, 1990) and William S. Kurz, *Reading Luke-Acts* (Louisville: Westminster/John Knox, 1993). A good survey of current Lukan scholarship is Mark Allen Powell, *What are they saying about Luke?* (New York: Paulist, 1989).

[38]This expression is found in Mark 1:4 as well but is never developed thematically in Mark.

[39]This expression is similar to Matt 3:8, but Luke never develops it into a major aspect of his understanding of conversion. Note Luke's plural "fruits," which emphasizes individual acts, as compared to Matthew's singular, which represents a broad metaphor for human action.

[40]Luke-Acts exhibits a special preference for describing the story of Jesus and the church as guided by the Holy Spirit (e.g., 1:15; 41; 4:1; Acts 1:2; 2:4, etc.).

[41]Mercy (*eleos*) is a quality which Luke attributes not only to God but which is also demanded of people, as is apparent in the example of the Good Samaritan (10:29-37).

[42]For a fuller exposition of the Lukan theme of salvation see Neal Flanagan, "The What and How of Salvation in Luke-Acts," in Daniel Durkin (ed.), *Sin, Salvation and the Spirit* (Collegeville: Liturgical, 1979) 203-13.

[43]This verse is curiously missing from some of the best manuscripts but clearly reflects the Lukan perspective.

⁴⁴Luke uses the vocabulary of sin, sinners, sinfulness much more frequently than Mark and Matthew (Dick 1984: 55), as a glance at a concordance shows.

⁴⁵For recent studies of the parables, see John R. Donahue, *The Gospel in Parable* (Philadelphia: Fortress, 1988) and Bernard Brandon Scott, *Hear Then the Parable* (Minneapolis: Fortress, 1989).

⁴⁶Luke's word for joy (1:14; 2:10; 24:52) comes from the same Greek root as the word for God's gracious favor (1:30; 2:40, 52). A study by J. Nolland (*NTS* 32 [1986] 614-20) indicates that Luke understands *charis* to be "a tangible, divine power dramatically present with Jesus and the church of Acts" (615).

⁴⁷The actual Greek word used here is the related verb *apostrephō*.

⁴⁸See Dupont (1979: 82) for a fuller explanation of this term.

⁴⁹*Pace* William H. Willimon, *Acts* (Interpretation Commentary; Atlanta: John Knox, 1988) 102. While their characterization is minimized, they become key markers in the geographical spread of the gospel in Acts.

⁵⁰Baptism by trinitarian formula (Father, Son, Holy Spirit) is a later development, but it is evident in Matthew 28:19.

⁵¹See most recently, Frank J. Matera, "Responsibility for the Death of Jesus according to the Acts of the Apostles," *JSNT* 39 (1990) 77-93.

⁵²The phrase "opened his mouth" in conjunction with "proclaimed (*euēggelisato*) Jesus" represents the formal witnessing of a disciple (cf. Acts 18:9; 22:14-15).

⁵³Ronald D. Witherup, " 'Functional Redundancy' in the Acts of the Apostles: A Case Study," *JSNT* 48 (1992) 67-86.

⁵⁴*The Habit of Being* (ed. Sally Fitzgerald; New York: Vintage, 1979) 355.

⁵⁵Most notably, Krister Stendahl, *Paul Among Jews and Gentiles and Other Essays* (Philadelphia: Fortress, 1986) 7-23.

⁵⁶The image of blindness/sight has important symbolic value in Luke-Acts, as Dennis Hamm has shown in two articles, "Sight to the Blind: Vision as Metaphor in Luke," *Bib* 67 (1986) 457-77, and "Paul's Blindness and Its Healing: Clues to Symbolic Intent (Acts 9; 22 and 26)" *Bib* 71 (1990) 63-72.

⁵⁷This word and its cognates are key Lukan concepts tied to discipleship (Luke 24:48; Acts 1:8; 2:32; 3:15; 5:32; 10:39, 41; 13:31).

⁵⁸For a full analysis of this passage see Ronald D. Witherup, "Cornelius Over and Over and Over Again: 'Functional Redundancy' in the Acts of the Apostles," *JSNT* 49 (1993) 45-66.

⁵⁹On hospitality in Luke-Acts, see John Koenig, *New Testament Hospitality: Partnership with Strangers as Promise and Mission* (Philadelphia: Fortress, 1985) 85-123.

[60]A "dealer in purple cloth" (Acts 16:14) is by definition in the NT rather wealthy because it was the color worn by royalty.

[61]See various testimonies recorded in William James, *The Varieties of Religious Experience* (Garden City, N.Y.: Doubleday, 1978) 250–53.

[62]The Letters of John are part of the Johannine literature and thus part of the perspective we seek. There is little concern in them about conversion *per se.* Consequently, they will be used more corroboratively.

[63]But see John 5:35 where John the Baptist is alluded to as a "shining lamp," a temporary light.

[64]This word and its cognates are favorite Johannine expressions for proclaiming God's truth to the world (for example, cf. 1:7–8, 15, 34; 3:11, 26, 28, 32; 8:14, 18; 10:25; 18:37; 19:35; 21:24).

[65]It is interesting to note that John 4:1–3 describes both John the Baptist and Jesus as involved in baptismal activity in Judea, and that this seems to have caused some controversy between the disciples of both men. But baptism is not explicitly connected here with conversion.

[66]It is characteristic of John to emphasize the relationship *individuals* have with Jesus (e.g., sheep to the shepherd, 10:14; branches to the vine, 15:5). It is essential for an individual to "remain" in Jesus as Jesus does in him or her (15:4, 6, 7). This is balanced by the strong communal dimension in the commands to "love one another" (15:12) and to be of service to one another (13:4–16).

[67]In John's Gospel Jesus normally accomplishes "signs" rather than miracles, and these signs are indicative of Jesus' identity and eschatological power as the one who has been "sent" by the Father (cf. 2:11; 4:48, 54; 6:2, 14, 26; 7:31; 9:16; 11:47; 12:18, 37; 20:30).

[68]"You" in this verse is plural but in verse 3 is singular. It indicates that the teaching is no longer directed only to Nicodemus, who disappears from the narrative once Jesus' monologue begins, but is directed to all the Christian community.

[69]In the NT this contrast appears also in James 1:17; 3:15, 17.

[70]See Raymond E. Brown, *The Gospel According to John I-XII* (AB 29; Garden City, N.Y.: Doubleday, 1966) 141–44.

[71]*Eternal* life refers not only to length of time but also quality of life (6:54; 10:28; 17:3).

[72]This motif is part of a developed "replacement theology" in John in which the presence of Jesus displaces traditional Jewish cult (e.g., 2:1–11; 6:22–51).

[73]Unlike the Synoptic Gospels where Jesus is sent to Israel, John's more cosmic view sees Jesus as sent to the world (1:10; 3:17; 9:39; 16:28; 18:37).

[74]See J. Warren Holleran, "Seeing the Light: A Narrative Reading of John 9" *ETL* 69 (1993), 5–26 and forthcoming. My own structuring of the passage, however, differs slightly from Holleran's proposal.

[75]The term "judgment" here is not referring to an eschatological judgment as in the Synoptic Gospels (e.g., Mark 13). John's Gospel has what scholars call "realized eschatology," emphasizing the judgment or the time of decision *now* (e.g., 12:31).

[76]It is difficult to explore any one aspect of Paul's theology without taking into account the "big picture." But we have limited space here. An excellent introduction to Paul's thought is Joseph A. Fitzmyer, *Paul and His Theology: A Brief Sketch* (Englewood Cliffs: Prentice-Hall, 1989).

[77]Romans, 1 and 2 Corinthians, Galatians, Philippians, 1 Thessalonians, and Philemon.

[78]Ephesians, Colossians, 2 Thessalonians, and the Pastoral Epistles (1, 2 Timothy and Titus).

[79]For a succinct summary of this issue, see Joseph Plevnik, *What are they saying about Paul?* (New York: Paulist, 1986) 55–76.

[80]See Plevnik, *What are they saying?* 5–27.

[81]Taking Romans 7:15–25 to refer to the interior conflict of a divided self is not to deny that Paul is speaking of the tyranny of sin as an *external* power that causes this dilemma. But the human person experiences this dilemma internally and is bewildered by it.

[82]Note that Acts usually does not refer to Paul as an "apostle" (Acts 14:14 is an exception). For Luke, the title applies only to the Twelve (and later to Matthias, Judas' replacement; Acts 1:26).

[83]Harold W. Attridge, *Hebrews* (Hermeneia; Philadelphia: Fortress, 1989) 167.

[84]Sophie Laws, *The Epistle of James* (San Francisco: Harper & Row, 1980) 239–41.

[85]An impassioned plea for this aspect of conversion is found in Jim Wallis, *The Call to Conversion: Recovering the Gospel for These Times* (San Francisco: Harper & Row, 1981).

[86]Flannery O'Connor, (Sally Fitzgerald [ed.]), *The Habit of Being* (New York: Farrar, Strauss, Giroux, 1979) 430.

[87]*Lumen gentium* #8, quoting St. Augustine.

[88]Quoted from Norman P. Tanner (ed.), *Decrees of the Ecumenical Councils,* Vol. II (London: Sheed & Ward; Washington: Georgetown University, 1990) 855–56.

[89]Tanner, *Decrees,* 912–13.